Arabella Boxer has written several cookbooks, notably First Slice Your Cookbook *and* Arabella Boxer's Garden Cookbook. *She has also written on food and gardening for* Nova *and* The Sunday Times *and worked for two years as cookery correspondent for* Vogue.

CHRISTMAS FOOD AND DRINK

Arabella Boxer

SPHERE BOOKS LIMITED
30/32 Gray's Inn Road, London WC1X 8JL

First published in Great Britain by Sphere Books Ltd 1975
Copyright © Arabella Boxer 1975

Set in Monotype Plantin

Printed in Great Britain by
Hazell Watson & Viney Ltd
Aylesbury, Bucks

RECIPES

**All the quantities given are intended to feed
five or six people unless otherwise stated**

INTRODUCTION

Of all the religious feasts, Christmas must be the most complex. Composed as it is of a subtle mixture of Christianity and paganism, with overtones of myth and superstition, it has become over the centuries a subtle and intricate blend of different themes. Above all, it is a perfect family occasion, as it can be interpreted and celebrated in so many different ways, according to the nature of the individual. For those who are so inclined, there are the beautiful and mysterious church services, the midnight masses and carol-singing; for those with more worldly tastes, there are the parties, the decorations and the glitter. For children, the mixture of presents, food and decoration seems specially designed to appeal to their own particular mixture of greed, materialism and fantasy. And there is the element of real warmth and generosity, of seeing friends and giving presents, extending hospitality as widely as finances permit. Because it is primarily a feast, food and drink have always played an important part in the Christmas scene. The rôle played by feasting is a special one, now far removed from its pagan origins, as for example in the *reveillon*, the lavish dinner traditionally prepared in most continental Catholic homes to greet the family and friends on their return from midnight mass, early on Christmas morning. Strangely enough, food plays little part in the English Church, unlike most other religions where an important holy day is almost always preceeded by fasting, and followed by a celebratory meal of some sort.

Luckily, Christmas festivities are ones that benefit from being prepared in advance, from the mixing of the pudding to the wrapping up of presents, and these repeated rituals often become the favourites of children. A certain amount of planning is almost essential if one is to survive a traditional Christmas, and I have found that even the most modest preparation – say, one cake made in advance – has a psychological effect of keeping panic at bay.

In our parents' days, the puddings were often made one year to be eaten the following, but I find this is only practicable in old-fashioned houses with large cool larders, plenty of room, and a good supply of mixing bowls, as half of them are permanently out of action. In centrally-heated houses with little or no storage space of a suitable temperature, the puddings tend to develop an unattractive layer of mould, probably quite safe, but hardly very appealing. I reckon late October or early November is a reasonable time to start making the puddings; one can be eaten right away, while the others are stored for Christmas itself. They are best made in largish quantities, so it seems sensible to have an arrangement with a friend or relative to take it in turns to make the puddings for both families. I find one rarely wants to eat the second or third, while even the first, if eaten shortly before Christmas, can spoil the pleasure on the day itself.

A rich plum cake can also be made in advance, stored carefully in an airtight tin, and only iced shortly before eating. Lady Moray's plum cake (see page 107) is perfect for this. Pickles and relishes are best made several weeks beforehand, and either eaten at Christmas to brighten up a meal of cold meat, or used as last-minute Christmas presents. Special labels can be made for the ones to be given away (see Jocasta Innes). Pâtés can be made a week or two before Christmas and used in the same way, either as food for the household or as presents. If they are to be kept longer than a week, or given away, they must be completely sealed with a layer of melted butter or lard, and stored in the bottom of the refrigerator. Those made within the week, however, can be finished off more elegantly, with decorations of herbs or bay leaves, as the fat is not necessary.

As Christmas grows nearer, the campaign starts in earnest with planning the meals and ordering the food. I usually believe in having one stand-by, a small boned ham, for instance, or half a large gammon. The former is particularly good as it keeps longer without the bone, and if wrapped in clean muslin and stored in the refrigerator will last for at least two weeks without becoming dry. A smoked turkey is a more unusual delicacy, but only to be considered if one's main Christmas meal is something quite different; a goose, perhaps, or a capon. A large joint of spiced beef prepared according to Elizabeth David's recipe can be bought from Harrods, along with cooking instructions, and is a delicious thing to fall back on for cold meals.

Instead of ordering a huge turkey and planning to make several meals from it, I now order a small turkey and eat off it only twice, once hot and a second time cold. Then I make a soup with the remains and avoid all the tiresome business of re-heating it in various ways.

During the week before, I try to make a good stock of salted almonds which are so delicious to eat with drinks, and a stock of biscuits. The American icebox cookies on pages 106–107 are excellent for this purpose as they are prepared in advance and only baked as required. If you have a deep freeze, it is a good idea to bake a few loaves of bread and freeze them to avoid the dreary stale bread which is otherwise inevitable. A fresh crusty loaf of home-made bread can make a simple meal of pâté and salad quite delicious. I have come to rely more and more on this sort of planning: stocking the freezer with New England or Bertorelli ice-cream, for example, and having a supply of home-made biscuits to eat with it, or a home-made sauce.

A good supply of fresh breadcrumbs can be made shortly before Christmas for the stuffings and puddings, while a large jar of vanilla sugar should be prepared well ahead of time for flavouring sweet sauces. I love making puddings at Christmas time, and try to remember to have a couple of extra white loaves of bread for that purpose. In recent years we have been urged so many times to stop eating puddings, and to end our meals with fruit or cheese, but fruit is so exorbitantly expensive in mid-winter, and good cheese so hard to find in the country, that I have started to revive the old puddings and find they are greeted with cries of joy by almost all my family and friends. It is certainly an economical way of feeding people, and a comforting end to a meal. A hot pudding is particularly welcome after a cold meal.

A small amount of concentrated meat glaze is a very valuable thing to have in the refrigerator for making oeufs au jus (just add a teaspoon of glaze to oeufs en cocotte) or as the base for sauces. Remembering there will be a plentiful supply of stock from the bird, it is good to think in terms of one or two soups and to lay in the other ingredients: plenty of onions, for example, and a good store of root vegetables – carrots, turnips, and parsnips.

Another useful thing to prepare in advance is a jug of sugar syrup for making old-fashioneds and other cocktails, while a bottle of sloe gin, made from sloes picked in the autumn is a marvellous treat to produce as a drink before lunch or dinner. This also makes an ideal Christmas present when bottled attractively with specially designed labels (see Jocasta Innes).

As I get older, I like to eat less and drink more, at Christmas time especially. I think that drink can play just as important a part as food in the festive scene, and causes a great deal less trouble. I now prefer to mix an elaborate cocktail instead of cooking a soup or first course for an evening meal – I find the sight of a loaded drinks tray with oranges and lemons and maraschino cherries is far more appealing to most adults' jaded eyes than yet more food.

Many of the cocktails I like to drink at Christmas time may seem more suited to summer drinking, but it must be remembered how over-fed and over-warmed and generally over-stimulated we usually are at Christmas time, and the cool sharp taste of a Campari cocktail, for example, can have a delicious astringent counter-effect.

Some years ago, we went to stay with a friend in Scotland for Christmas, and each evening her father would mix old-fashioneds for us all. These still seem to me the ideal Christmas drink – short, strong, and lovely to look at with the orange, lemon and cherry floating with the ice cubes in the golden bourbon. Whiskey cocktails seem the perfect winter drink, and for this bourbon (or rye) is essential, as the unmistakable smoky taste of scotch does not blend well with other tastes, except possibly ginger ale. Cocktails made with white rum, such as daiquiris, are also delicious and pretty with the red of the cherry gleaming through the opaque white liquid. For a more special effect, the rims of the glasses can be frosted (see page 120).

As an aperitif before lunch, I think sloe gin is one of the best of all winter drinks, and if it is one's own home-made brand, so much the better. Cherry brandy is also excellent occasionally, and very warming when drunk out-of-doors. I also include one or two recipes for mulled wines; once or twice a year these taste excellent, especially when you come in chilled from out-of-doors. There are a few cups, too, which I like to have for family parties as it is easy to vary the strength according to the age of the guests without being in the least obvious, and because they look so jolly.

Lastly comes the subject of champagne. Those who really love champagne cannot bear to see it made into cocktails and cups, and good champagne is certainly too expensive to fool about with. Many harsh words are said about the vulgarity of the champagne cocktail, but for me it will always have a certain glamour – as a child it seemed to me the height of sophistication and – albeit Hollywood – romance, so I include a recipe for that, too.

Before the holiday season starts, I should lay in a good supply of fresh oranges, lemons, and limes when available; a jar of maraschino cherries, some cocktail sticks, some lump and some castor sugar. I would then prepare a jug of sugar syrup (see page 116) and store it in the refrigerator. I would also lay in a bottle of bourbon, one of Bacardi White Label rum, a bottle of Campari, one of sweet white Cinzano, a half-bottle of orange curaçao and one of Cointreau, some bottles of fizzy mineral water such as Vichy or Perrier – so much better than soda water for making cups – and some bottles of red claret-type wine and of white Rhein wine, Sauternes or Moselle. Also useful are some angostura bitters, and some stick cinnamon and whole nutmeg and whole cloves for flavouring spiced wine. With these in the drinks cupboard, and possibly a jar of salted almonds, I feel well set up for the festive season, and capable of throwing together any number of cocktails, cups or punches at a moment's notice.

CHART OF CHRISTMAS PREPARATIONS

1 The First Part – any time between late October and mid-November

1 Make the Christmas puddings.
2 Make the Christmas cake.
3 Prepare a large jar of vanilla sugar.
4 Make pickles, relishes, preserves, e.g. Cumberland Sauce, prunes in wine, raspberry vodka, etc.

2 The Second Part – the beginning of Christmas week

1 Make pâtés.
2 Make biscuits.
3 Make cranberry sauce.
4 Make brandy butter.
5 Plan meals for the whole holiday period.
6 Order the food to be delivered.
7 Make salted almonds.
8 Make sugar syrup.

3 The Third Part – Christmas Eve

1 Make lots of white breadcrumbs.
2 Make the stuffings.
3 Start the giblet gravy.
4 Weigh the turkey and calculate the cooking time.
5 Find a pot to fit the pudding.
6 Lay the table.
7 Make a supply of fruit juice.
8 Prepare dishes for second Christmas meal.
9 Look out all relevant recipes.

4 The Day Itself – Christmas morning

1 Turn on oven.
2 Put water on to boil for pudding.
3 Stuff turkey and prepare for oven.
4 Put pudding on to steam.

5 Put bird in oven.

6 Shell chestnuts.

7 Prepare vegetables.

8 Put on milk for bread sauce.

9 Finish making giblet gravy.

10 Turn turkey twice during cooking.

11 Watch pudding during cooking.

12 Cook chestnuts.

13 Heat plates and dishes.

14 Cook vegetables.

15 Cook any extras such as tiny sausages, bacon rolls, forcemeat balls, etc.

16 Baste turkey during final browning.

17 Make bread sauce.

18 Don't forget cranberry sauce and brandy butter in refrigerator.

19 Later, turn out pudding and ignite with brandy.

SUGGESTED MENUS FOR HOLIDAY

Christmas Eve – dinner
Turbot or halibut gratin; purée of potatoes; broccoli
Castle puddings

Christmas Day – luncheon
Roast turkey, goose, or capon; purée of potatoes; brussels sprouts;
bread sauce and/or cranberry sauce; sausages; bacon rolls; etc.
Plum pudding; brandy butter

Dinner
Vegetable consommé
Cold ham and Cumberland Sauce; salad
Prune jelly or yoghurt

Boxing Day – lunch
Cold turkey; baked potatoes; salad
Mince pies; brandy butter

Dinner
Smoked haddock Monte Carlo; rice; lettuce salad
Wine jelly

The day after Boxing Day – lunch
Beef stewed in cider; haricot beans; green salad
Blazing apples

Dinner
Onion soup made from turkey stock
Noodles with poppy seeds; green salad
Raspberry meringue

Alternative menu plan for Christmas Day with the main meal in the evening

Christmas Day – lunch
Cold ham; baked potatoes; salad
Apple fritters

Dinner
A clear soup, either tinned turtle soup with a little sherry, or vegetable
consommé with cheese biscuits
Roast turkey, etc.

ORDERING THE FOOD

1 To be ordered well in advance i.e. late November

The turkey, goose, or capon.

A small boned ham, cooked, *or* ½ a cooked ham or gammon, *or* a joint of spiced beef, *or* a smoked turkey.

2 To be ordered at the beginning of Christmas week

(a) From the butcher

Sausage meat; sausages; bacon; 2½ lb stewing beef.

(b) From the greengrocer

Plenty of potatoes and onions; some carrots and leeks; a few turnips and parsnips. Plenty of salad vegetables: lettuce, batavia, chicory, endive, watercress, cucumber, fennel; 2 lb brussels sprouts; 1½ lb broccoli; some tomatoes. Some cooking apples; plenty of eating apples, tangerines, etc. Plenty of oranges and lemons, limes if available.

(c) From the grocer:

Lots of eggs, plenty of butter and some cream.

(d) From the fishmonger

2 lb turbot or halibut, 2 large smoked haddocks.

SOUPS

AMERICAN BOILED DINNER
BEAN SOUP
BEETROOT SOUP
CABBAGE SOUP WITH YOGHURT
CHESTNUT SOUP
COCK-A-LEEKIE
CURRIED FISH SOUP
FISH CHOWDER
GAME SOUP WITH LENTILS
NUT SOUP
ONION SOUP
PARSNIP SOUP
A SIMPLE POT-AU-FEU
RUSSIAN SOUP
VEGETABLE BROTH
VEGETABLE CONSOMME

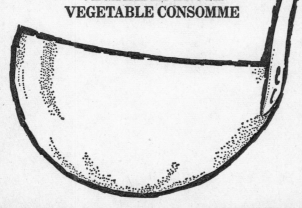

We were to have a superb dinner, consisting of a leg of pickled pork and greens, and a pair of roast stuffed fowls. A handsome mince-pie had been made yesterday morning, and the pudding was already on the boil. These extensive arrangements occasioned us to be cut off unceremoniously in respect of breakfast; 'for I an't,' said Mrs Joe, 'I an't a-going to have no formal cramming and bursting and washing up now, with what I've got before me, I promise you!'

PIP'S CHRISTMAS DINNER, *GREAT EXPECTATIONS*, CHARLES DICKENS, 1861

AMERICAN BOILED DINNER

1 lb streaky bacon in one piece
1 boiling fowl cut in pieces
1 onion
2 leeks
1 stalk celery
1 bay leaf
1 sprig thyme
sea salt and black peppercorns
2 large carrots
1 cabbage

Put the bacon and the chicken pieces in a deep pot and cover with cold water. Bring to the boil and skim off the scum that rises to the surface. When the surface is clear, put in the onion, celery, bay leaf, thyme, some sea salt and 10 black peppercorns. Simmer for 1¾ hours, then put in the leeks and carrots cut in thick slices, and the cabbage cut in quarters. Bring back to the boil and simmer for another ¾ hour. Take out the bacon, remove the rind and cut in slices. Cut the chicken off the bones. Put some bacon and chicken in each soup plate, add some leeks and carrots (discard the onion and celery) and pour the soup over all. Serve with soup spoons, knives and forks. For an even more substantial meal, add a dish of plain boiled potatoes. An excellent one-dish meal, this can also be re-heated very successfully.

BEAN SOUP

6 oz dried haricot beans (cannellini
    or soissons if possible)
1 onion
2 carrots
2 leeks
2 stalks celery
½ lb tomatoes
4 Tbs olive oil
2½ pt game stock, or the bean stock
    mixed with some chicken stock
1 dessertspoon sea salt
black pepper
4 Tbs chopped parsley

Soak the dried beans for 2–3 hours, then cook in fresh water until soft. Drain them and reserve the stock. Chop the onion, carrots, leeks and celery and keep in separate piles. Heat the oil in a casserole and cook the onion in it slowly until slightly softened. Add the carrots, then the leeks, then the celery. Skin the tomatoes, chop them and add last of all. Heat the stock and pour on. Bring to the boil and simmer gently for about 25 minutes, till the vegetables are soft without being mushy. Stir in the beans and re-heat. Add salt and pepper, and stir in the chopped parsley.

When made in conjunction with a game pâté, using the carcase of the almost raw pheasant for the stock, this is the best soup imaginable. Otherwise it can be made with chicken stock, or simply with the cooking liquor from the beans made up to the right amount, with a $\frac{1}{2}$ stock cube added.

BEETROOT SOUP

$1\frac{1}{2}$ lb raw beetroot
1 large onion
3 carrots
3 stalks celery

2 pt beef or duck stock, made with a cube if necessary
salt and pepper
$\frac{1}{4}$ pt sour cream
lemon juice or wine vinegar

Scrub the beetroot and cut in chunks. Put in a large pan with the onion, carrots and celery, all cut in pieces. Cover with the cold stock and bring slowly to the boil, adding salt and black pepper. Remove any scum that rises to the surface and when boiling point is reached lower the heat and cover the pan. Simmer gently for about 50 minutes, or till the beetroots are soft. Throw away the onion, carrots and celery. Pour the liquid soup through a vegetable mill and push through just enough of the cooked beetroot to give the consistency you want. (If a clear soup is required, use the liquid only). Re-heat, adding more salt and pepper to taste. The sour cream can be stirred in at this stage, or handed separately. If it is to be eaten cold, strain off the liquid and chill in the refrigerator after adjusting seasoning. Add lemon juice (or a little vinegar) to sharpen the flavour.

CABBAGE SOUP WITH YOGHURT

1 large onion
2 oz butter
$\frac{1}{2}$ lb tomatoes
2 pt stock, beef or chicken
2 oz barley

1 small green cabbage, or 1 lb chard, kale, or spinach beet
sea salt and black pepper
$\frac{1}{2}$ pt yoghurt

Chop the onion and cook gently in the butter till soft. Skin the tomatoes, chop them, and add to the onion. Stew gently for about 4 minutes, then heat the stock and pour on. Bring it to the boil and put in the barley – I prefer the pot barley bought in health shops to pearl barley, but either will do – which should be soaked for two or three hours if possible. Simmer with the lid on for 30 minutes. Take the heart of the cabbage, about 1 lb in weight, and chop it quite finely. Add it to the soup and cook for another 30 minutes. Beat the yoghurt till smooth in a bowl, stir in a ladleful of the hot soup, then return the mixture to the pot. Stir carefully till re-heated, without allowing it to boil or the yoghurt will curdle. Season to taste with sea salt and black pepper.

A delicious soup with a fresh lemony taste; filling, without being heavy.

CHESTNUT SOUP

½ lb chestnuts
1 medium onion
1 carrot
1 leek
1 stalk celery

1 cooking apple
2 pt game, chicken, or meat stock
sea salt and black pepper
2 Tbs chopped parsley

Shell the nuts by first making a nick in each one with a small sharp knife. Put them in a pan and cover with cold water. Bring to the boil and remove from the heat. Lift out the nuts, three or four at a time, and take off the shells with the same knife. Keep the other ones as hot as possible. Put the shelled nuts in a pan with the sliced onion, carrot, leek and celery. Cover with the stock, add salt and pepper, and bring to the boil. Simmer for 30 minutes, then add the peeled and chopped apple. Simmer another 10 minutes, till all is soft, then put through the medium mesh of the vegetable mill, or the blender if you like a very smooth soup. Return to the clean pan, re-heat and add more salt and pepper as needed. Sprinkle with chopped parsley and serve. Serves 6–8. A filling and delicious soup.

COCK-A-LEEKIE

1 boiling fowl
6 leeks
1 large carrot
1 large onion

2 bay leaves
a dessertspoon sea salt
10 black peppercorns
4 Tbs chopped parsley

Put the chicken in a deep pot with the onion and carrot cut in halves, and the bay leaves. Cover with cold water and bring slowly to the boil. Skim off any froth on the surface, and add the salt and the peppercorns. Cover the pan and cook very gently for 2 hours. Then take out the onion, carrot and bay leaves and put in the leeks, cut in thick diagonal slices, about 2 inches across. Bring back to the boil and simmer for another hour. Take out the chicken and cut the flesh off the bone into small pieces. Put these in a soup tureen with the leeks and pour over enough of the soup to fill the bowl — there should be enough left to make another dish the following day. Sprinkle with the chopped parsley.

Serve with a dish of boiled rice and eat in soup plates. This makes a complete meal for about 8 people.

CURRIED FISH SOUP

1 halibut steak, $\frac{1}{2}$–$\frac{3}{4}$ lb, plus head,
  tail, etc.
1 carrot
1 leek
1 bay leaf
3 sprigs parsley
6 black peppercorns
1 dessertspoon sea salt

$1\frac{1}{2}$ Tbs wine vinegar
1 Tbs curry powder
4 Tbs ground almonds
2 onions
2 oz butter
1 oz rice
$\frac{1}{2}$ gill cream

Make a stock by putting the halibut head, tail, etc. in a pan with the carrot, leek, bay leaf, parsley, peppercorns, salt and vinegar. Cover with cold water. Boil all together for 1 hour, then strain and leave to cool. You will need $1\frac{3}{4}$ pints, so reduce if too much. Make the almond milk by pouring $\frac{3}{4}$ pint of the strained fish stock, re-heated until boiling, over the ground almonds and leaving to infuse for 30 minutes. Chop the onions and cook gently until soft and golden in the butter. Add the curry powder and cook a few minutes longer. Pour on 1 pint of the strained fish stock and bring to the boil. Add the almond milk – do not strain it – and the cream. Simmer until smooth. Cook the rice in boiling salted water; grill the halibut steak and flake the flesh. Put the rice and the halibut flakes in a tureen and pour the soup over them. Serves 6–8. An extremely good soup, rich and filling.

FISH CHOWDER

1 oz butter, melted
1 onion
1½ lb fresh haddock fillet
1 lb potatoes

2 oz streaky bacon rashers (or 3 Tbs chopped parsley)
sea salt and black pepper
½ pt thin cream

Put the melted butter in the bottom of a heavy casserole. Chop the onion finely and put in the casserole. Skin the fish fillets and cut them in neat pieces. Lay them on top of the onion. Peel the potatoes and slice them about ¼ inch thick. Lay the slices over the fish, seasoning each layer with sea salt and black pepper. Add enough cold water to just cover the surface of the potatoes and bring to the boil. Cover the pan and simmer gently for 40 minutes. When the potatoes are cooked, heat the cream and pour in. Stir very gently to mix without breaking up the pieces of fish and the potato slices, and season with more salt and pepper as needed. Chop the bacon rashers and fry gently until crisp, scatter over the top and serve with water biscuits – Jewish Matzos are best. Alternatively, the fried bacon can be replaced by 3 Tbs finely chopped parsley. A meal in itself, this dish should be served in soup plates, and only needs a salad to follow it.

GAME SOUP WITH LENTILS

1 pheasant carcase
2 onions
2 carrots
2 leeks
3 stalks celery

1 bay leaf
1 dessertspoon sea salt
10 black peppercorns
3 Tbs olive oil
½ lb brown (continental) lentils

This excellent soup can be made at the same time as a game pâté, using most of the meat for the pâté. It can also be made with the remains of a roast bird, although this does not give such a good flavour as the first method. Pick as much meat off the carcase as you can, and reserve it. Put the bones in a pan with 1 onion, 1 carrot, 1 leek, 1 stalk celery, a bay leaf, the sea salt and peppercorns. Cover with plenty of cold water and bring slowly to the boil. Simmer gently for 2–3 hours, then strain and cool. You will need 2½–3 pints. Chop the remaining vegetables and heat the oil in a casserole. Cook the onion in it until it turns transparent and starts to soften. Add the carrot, leek and celery. Stew gently for about 8 minutes, then add the washed lentils. Stir around until coated with oil and well mixed, then pour on the heated stock, having removed as much fat as possible from the surface. Simmer gently for 45 minutes or till the lentils are soft. Chop the reserved scraps of pheasant and add to the soup. (If these are from the raw carcase, add them 5 minutes before the end of the simmering to allow them to cook through.) Add sea salt and freshly ground black pepper to taste. Serves 6–8.

NUT SOUP

¼ lb peanuts
2½ pt chicken or beef stock (can be made from a cube)
1 large onion
2 leeks
½ lb tomatoes
6 oz button mushrooms
sea salt and black pepper

Grind the nuts in the liquidiser or in a cheese grater. Put them in a large saucepan with ½ pt of the stock. Bring to the boil and simmer gently for 10 minutes, stirring often. Add the sliced onion and leeks and the rest of the stock. Simmer for 20 minutes, then add the skinned and chopped tomatoes and the sliced mushrooms. Bring back to the boil and simmer for another 15 minutes, adding more stock if it becomes too thick. Season with salt and pepper and serve. An excellent soup, unusual and very nourishing. It can be made a day in advance and re-heated.

ONION SOUP

2 lb large mild onions
2 oz butter
2 pt turkey stock

sea salt and black pepper
1 Tbs brandy (optional)

Slice the onions and cook gently in the butter until slightly softened and pale golden. Heat the stock and pour on. Simmer for 35 minutes, adding salt and pepper to taste. Add a drop of brandy, or sherry, if liked.

PARSNIP SOUP

4 oz streaky bacon rashers
1 oz butter
1 large onion
2 stalks celery
1 lb parsnips
1 bay leaf

sea salt and black pepper
1½ Tbs flour
1 pt creamy milk
½ oz butter
4 Tbs chopped parsley

Chop the bacon and fry gently in 1 oz butter in a heavy pan. Allow about 10 minutes slow frying for the bacon to render all its fat and become crisp. Chop the onion and add it to the bacon, adding a little extra fat if necessary. Cook gently, stirring often for another 8–10 minutes, till the onion has softened. Chop the celery and add to the pan. Cook another 6–8 minutes – the chopped parsnips cook so quickly that the other vegetables must be three-quarters cooked before adding them, otherwise the soup will become mushy before the onion and celery are tender. Peel the parsnips and chop them. Add to the celery and onion and barely cover with hot water. Add a bay leaf, sea salt and black pepper, remembering the bacon is already salty, and simmer for 10–12 minutes, till the parsnips are soft. Mix the flour to a paste in a cup with a little of the milk, and stir into the soup. Simmer for 2 minutes till slightly thickened, then heat the rest of the milk and pour on. When all is well mixed and hot, stir in the ½ oz butter, then the chopped parsley, and serve. A delicious and unusual soup.

A SIMPLE POT-AU-FEU

2 lb leg of beef	1 bay leaf
1 large onion	3 stalks parsley
4 large carrots	2 tsp sea salt
4 large leeks	8 black peppercorns

Cut the beef in large square pieces, trimming off all fat. Place the meat in a casserole with 1 onion, 1 carrot and 1 leek, cut in quarters. Add the bay leaf and the parsley. Cover with cold water and place over gentle heat. Bring very slowly to the boil, allowing about 45 minutes to reach simmering point. When a brown scum starts to rise to the surface, remove it carefully. Spend several minutes doing this, as it is extremely important and cannot be left to the end. Add a cup of cold water and skim again. Then add a little salt and some black peppercorns and cover the pan. (Remember that it will concentrate during the long cooking and so do not add too much seasoning at this stage.) Simmer very gently for 5 hours, adding more boiling water if necessary. During the last half hour, cut the remaining carrots and leeks in thick slices and boil in a separate pan. When the pot-au-feu is ready, take out the meat and divide it between six soup plates. Add some freshly cooked carrots and leeks to each plate and cover with some of the delicious soup. (If the meat was properly trimmed of fat at the start, it will not need de-greasing.) Serve with a crusty loaf of fresh bread. With a salad and some cheese to follow, this makes a simple and delicious meal.

RUSSIAN SOUP

1 celeriac	1½ oz butter
1 onion	3 pt beef stock
1 leek	¼ pt sour cream
1 carrot	fresh dill or fennel, when available,
1 beetroot	or parsley
1 small green cabbage	sea salt and black pepper
¼ lb mushrooms	

Cut all the vegetables in thin strips like matchsticks. Melt the butter in a deep pot and cook the onion and leek in it till they soften. Put in all the other vegetables and stir round till well mixed. Stew them gently for 5 minutes, stirring occasionally. Heat the stock (use beef stock cubes if necessary, but weaker than directed) and pour into the pot. Bring to boiling point, cover the pan, and simmer gently for 1½ hours. Adjust seasoning, stir in the sour cream, and sprinkle with finely chopped dill or fennel (the herb, not the root) when available, or parsley. Serves 8.

VEGETABLE BROTH

2½ pt chicken or beef stock (made
    with a cube if necessary)
¼ lb very small onions
4 small leeks
½ lb small carrots
4 courgettes

6 small tomatoes
sea salt and black pepper
1 packet saffron (optional) or 3 Tbs
    chopped parsley
rice, couscous or kasha

Put the stock in a deep bowl with the peeled onions, the leeks cut in thick slices, and the carrots also cut in thick slices unless they are very small when they can be left whole. Add plenty of sea salt and bring to the boil. Simmer for 30 minutes, then add the courgettes cut in thick slices and cook for another 10 minutes after boiling point is regained. Peel the tomatoes and add them to the soup. After 5 minutes it should be ready. Add more salt and pepper to taste and stir in the saffron if you like it, or sprinkle with chopped parsley. To make this nourishing soup into a complete meal, serve with a dish of boiled rice, couscous or kasha, and let each guest help himself. Serve the soup in a large tureen and have soup plates to eat it in.

VEGETABLE CONSOMME

3 pt beef stock, made from bones
    and 1 lb cheap cut of beef
2 bay leaves
1 onion
1 leek
2 carrots

3 stalks celery
½ lb tomatoes
a small bunch watercress
a small head fennel (optional)
sea salt and black pepper
a little lemon juice

Make the beef stock the previous day, by covering beef or veal bones with plenty of cold water. Add 1 lb skirt of beef or other cheap cut, cut in small pieces, 1 onion and 2 bay leaves, and bring very slowly to the boil. When boiling point is reached, skim continuously for several minutes, till no more dark scum rises to the surface, then add a handful of sea salt and cover the pan. Simmer for 5–6 hours, watching from time to time to see the bones are still covered. Add more boiling water by degrees if necessary. When ready, pour the soup through a colander and leave to cool. Place in the refrigerator overnight. The next day, remove the fat from the surface, and measure 3 pints into a large saucepan. Scrub the vegetables and chop them in small pieces. Put them in the pot with the stock, bring slowly to the boil and simmer for 1½ hours. Strain the consommé and re-heat, adding salt, black pepper, and a little lemon juice to taste. Serve with hot cheese straws (see page 112). Makes about 2¼ pints, serves 6. A delicious fresh taste after too many rich meals.

PATES

DUCK PATE
KIPPER PATE
PHEASANT AND CHESTNUT PATE
SMOKED SALMON PATE

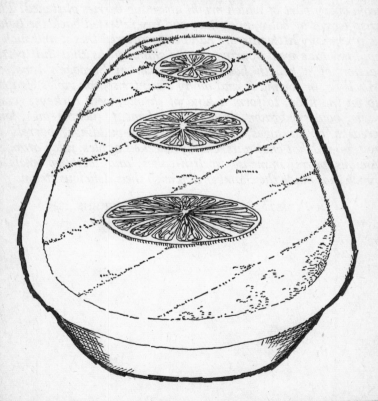

It was his own room. There was no doubt about that. But it had undergone a surprising transformation. The walls and ceiling were so hung with living green that it looked a perfect grove, from every part of which bright gleaming berries glistened. The crisp leaves of holly, mistletoe, and ivy reflected back the light, as if so many little mirrors had been scattered there; and such a mighty blaze went roaring up the chimney, as that dull petrifaction of a hearth had never known in Scrooge's time, or Marley's, or for many and many a winter season gone. Heaped up on the floor, to form a kind of throne, were turkeys, geese, game, poultry, brawn, great joints of meat, sucking-pigs, long wreaths of sausages, mince-pies, plum-puddings, barrels of oysters, red-hot chestnuts, cherry-cheeked apples, juicy oranges, luscious pears, immense twelfth-cakes, and seething bowls of punch that made the chamber dim with their delicious steam.

A CHRISTMAS CAROL, CHARLES DICKENS, 1843

DUCK PATE

1 duck
¾ lb fat pork; belly or throat
¾ lb veal
4 oz fat mild bacon
2 small oranges
10 black peppercorns

½ Tbs sea salt
1 clove garlic
½ tsp quatre-épices or mace
6 fl oz dry white wine
2 Tbs brandy

Ask your butcher to put the pork, veal and bacon through the mincer for you. Cook the duck for 25 minutes at 375°, then remove from the oven and leave to cool. When quite cold, cut all the flesh off the bones, removing the skin, and chop finely by hand. Chop the raw liver also. Mix the chopped duck with the minced meats and add the crushed peppercorns, sea salt and quatre-épices or mace and the crushed garlic. Moisten with the white wine and brandy, and add the juice of 1 orange. Taste for seasoning (make a tiny ball of the mixture and fry in butter). If possible, leave for an hour or two for the flavours to merge. Peel the remaining orange and slice thinly. Lay three or four of the slices in the bottom of your tin and spoon the mixture on top, flattening with a palette knife. Cook in a baking tin half full of water for 1½–1¾ hours at 310°. When cooked, the sides will have shrunk away from the sides of the tin. (Alternatively, divide between two tins and cook for 1¼–1½ hours.) Leave to cool then weight with two 2 lb weights, side by side. Put in the refrigerator when cold, and leave for at least one day before eating. It will keep up to one week perfectly well, or longer if you seal the top with pure lard to form an air-tight seal, in which case it can be kept for months. Serves 8.

KIPPER PATE

1 packet frozen kipper fillets
about 3 oz unsalted butter
2–3 Tbs thick cream

1 lemon
black pepper

Cook the kipper fillets as directed and drain well. When they have cooled, weigh them, then chop the flesh finely. If you have a mortar, pound the chopped flesh in it until smooth, otherwise bash it with a wooden spoon in a pudding basin to a paste. Add half its weight in slightly softened unsalted butter cut in small pieces. Work this into the fish until a smooth mixture is obtained. Add a little cream, and flavour carefully with lemon juice to taste. Add plenty of freshly ground black pepper; salt will not be needed. Fill a small bowl with the paste and level the top with a palette knife. Chill for several hours and serve with a tiny sprig of parsley on top. Accompany with toast and butter. If you want a really smooth pâté, and have the patience, the whole mixture can be pushed through a sieve at the end.

PHEASANT AND CHESTNUT PATE

1 pheasant
1½ lb belly of pork, or other cut of fat pork
¼ lb fat green bacon
2 cloves garlic
1 dessertspoon sea salt
10 black peppercorns
10 juniper berries
5–6 oz cooked chestnuts (allow ½ lb raw chestnuts)
2 Tbs brandy
6 fl oz red or white wine
some thin strips of bacon fat

Put the pheasant in a quick oven – 400° – for 15 minutes, then leave to cool. Cut the meat off the bones leaving a few scraps if you are going to make game soup (see page 22) with the remains. Chop the meat finely by hand. Get the butcher to put the pork and the bacon through his mincer for you if possible, otherwise do it yourself. Mix the chopped pheasant with the minced meats and add the crushed garlic, sea salt, the peppercorns and the juniper berries which you have crushed roughly in a mortar. Put aside for the flavours to develop while you prepare the chestnuts. Shell in the usual way (see page 19) and put the nuts in a small pan with some stock if you have any, or water, and cook for about 8 minutes till tender. Drain and cool. Chop them roughly when they have cooled and add to the meat mixture. Mix thoroughly and add the brandy and the wine. Try out for seasoning by frying a tiny ball. It should be quite highly seasoned; there is nothing worse than a bland pâté. Decorate two ovenproof dishes (or moulds) with the strips of bacon fat and divide the mixture between the two. Cook them in a baking tin half filled with water, uncovered, for 1¼–1½ hours at 310°. When cooked, the pâtés will have shrunk away from the sides of the dishes. Leave to cool for a couple of hours, then weight with some 2–3 lb weights, heavy tins, etc. The next day, store in the refrigerator, where they will keep for a week, or months if they have a completely air-tight seal of melted lard poured over them. To serve, remove the fat and turn them out onto a dish with their jelly round them. Serve with toast, or home-made bread. Each pâté will serve 6. Alternatively, one huge pâté can be made, increasing the cooking time by about 20 minutes. This will serve about 12. For a special treat, serve with home-made Cumberland sauce.

If giving these pâtés as Christmas presents, they can be made to look especially pretty by decorating (in the bottom of the dish, before piling in the pâté mixture) with a sprig of holly, made of small bay leaves and cranberries.

SMOKED SALMON PATE

4 oz smoked salmon pieces
   (trimmings are ideal for this
   dish)
2 oz unsalted butter

2 Tbs thick cream
black pepper
cayenne
lemon juice

Chop the smoked salmon, removing all hard pieces, bones, etc. Pound in a mortar till smooth, then add the butter cut in small pieces. The butter should be cool and firm, but not too hard. When all is amalgamated into a smooth paste, add the cream, plenty of freshly ground black pepper, cayenne and lemon juice to taste. Turn into a small dish and chill for several hours. Serve garnished with a sprig of parsley, with hot toast. Serves 2–3.

PASTA AND EGG DISHES

EGGS IN MACARONI CHEESE
CURRIED EGGS
NOODLES WITH POPPY SEEDS
SPAGHETTI ALLA CARBONARA
SPAGHETTI WITH VEGETABLE SAUCE
VERMICELLI SOUFFLE

CHRISTMAS DINNER

Turtle soup

2 *Fishes*

Turbot à la Vatel   Fillets of soles à la Tartare

3 *Removes*

Roast turkey   Braised ham à la jardinière
Périgueux sauce

4 *Entrées*

Marrow patties   Sweetbreads à la St Cloud
Salmis of pheasants   Mutton cutlets à la Vicomtesse
à la financière

SECOND COURSE

Woodcocks   (2 *Roasts*)   Grouse

Mince pies   (2 *Removes*)   Plum pudding

6 *Entremets*

Broccoli with Parmesan   Italian cream
cheese   Croûtes à l'ananas
Salad à la Rachel   Meringue à la Parisienne
Punch jelly

FRANCATELLI'S COOK'S GUIDE, London, 1884

EGGS IN MACARONI CHEESE

6 oz macaroni
6 eggs
6 thin slices ham
1½ oz butter

2 rounded Tbs flour
1 pt milk
¼ pt thin cream
5 oz grated Gruyère

Cook the macaroni. Boil the eggs for 5 minutes exactly (boil the water first) then cool and shell them. Melt the butter, stir in the flour and blend with the heated milk. Add the cream and 4 oz of the grated cheese. Mix with the macaroni. Wrap each of the eggs carefully in a slice of ham. Pour a thin layer of the macaroni into a shallow dish, lay the eggs-in-ham on it, and cover with the rest of the macaroni. Sprinkle with the remaining grated cheese and put in a quick oven – 400° – for 15 minutes, till golden brown on top and re-heated all through. Alternatively, if everything is kept hot, it may be simply browned under the grill. Serve with a lettuce salad.

CURRIED EGGS

1 medium onion
2 oz butter
1 Tbs curry powder (Spice Islands or Sea Isle if possible)
1 Tbs flour
¾ pt vegetable stock

¼ pt thin cream
1½ Tbs lemon juice
1½ Tbs orange juice
2 oz chopped (or nibbed) almonds
8 eggs

Chop the onion and cook till golden in the butter. Add the curry powder and the flour and cook gently for 2 minutes, then pour on the heated stock. Stir till blended and simmer for 15 minutes. Stir in the cream, then the lemon and orange juice. Add the nuts and mix well. Hard-boil the eggs, shell them and cut them into chunks, add to the sauce and re-heat gently. Serve with boiled rice and a fruit pickle or chutney.

NOODLES WITH POPPY SEEDS

1 lb noodles
4 oz butter

3 oz toasted breadcrumbs
1½ Tbs poppy seeds

Fry the breadcrumbs till nutty and brown in 3 oz butter. When almost ready, add the poppy seeds for the last minute or two. Cook the noodles as usual, drain well and stir in remaining butter. Add the breadcrumbs and poppy seeds, toss well and serve.

SPAGHETTI ALLA CARBONARA

1½ lb spaghetti
4–5 oz grated Parmesan
2 eggs, plus 2 yolks
3 oz butter

6 oz streaky bacon rashers
¼ pt thick cream
coarsely ground black pepper

Put a large pan of water on to boil for the spaghetti. While it is heating, prepare the sauce. Grate the cheese and put 3 oz apart. Cut the bacon in thin strips. While the spaghetti is cooking, beat the eggs and the yolks together, and stir in the 3 oz grated cheese. Cut the butter in small pieces. Fry the bacon strips in a frying pan until crisp; drain off most of the fat and pour in the cream. Heat and season with ground black pepper. When the spaghetti is tender, drain and turn into a hot serving bowl. Mix in the butter, then stir in the hot bacon and cream mixture. Pour the eggs and cheese over the top and mix with two large spoons. All this must be done very quickly, and everything must be as hot as possible – the spaghetti, the bowl, the bacon and cream. The eggs are cooked by the heat of the spaghetti, so if allowed to become cool it will not work. Serve immediately, with the extra cheese in a bowl on the table, and a pepper mill.

SPAGHETTI WITH VEGETABLE SAUCE

1½ lb spaghetti
1 large onion
2 large carrots
3 leeks
2 stalks celery
1½ lb tomatoes or a 14 oz tin
2 cloves garlic

½ lb button mushrooms
½ pt stock (if needed)
about 3 oz butter
2 tsp flour (if needed)
about 4 Tbs sunflower seed or nut
    oil

Chop the onion and cook in 2 oz butter and 3 Tbs oil in a large heavy casserole. Chop the carrots and par-boil for 5 minutes in lightly salted water. Drain, reserving the water if you have no stock. Chop the celery and leeks and add to the onion. Crush the garlic and add that also, then the drained carrots. Add more butter and oil if necessary. Skin and chop the tomatoes and add them to the pan. Cover and simmer gently for 15–20 minutes, stirring now and then. If the tomatoes are not very juicy, you may need to add some stock. Alternatively, if they are very watery you may need to thicken the liquid at the end of the cooking by stirring in a paste made from mixing 2 tsp flour and 1 Tbs butter. Drop into the pan in small bits and simmer, stirring, till smooth and thickened. If using tinned tomatoes, reserve most of the juice and only add as required. Cut the mushrooms in quarters and toss in butter till softened. Add them to the sauce at the end. Serve with 1½ lb spaghetti, freshly boiled and drained. Half a cooked chicken can be chopped and added to the sauce, or a whole chicken can be cooked especially, a few hours beforehand, the stock used for the sauce and the chopped meat stirred in at the end. Alternatively, a separate dish of meatballs can be served with the spaghetti and the vegetable sauce.

VERMICELLI SOUFFLE

¼ lb vermicelli
½ lb tomatoes
2 oz butter
2 Tbs flour
⅓ pt milk

3 oz grated Parmesan
sea salt and black pepper
3 egg yolks
4 egg whites
paprika

Cook the vermicelli in boiling salted water and drain well. Skin and chop the tomatoes. Cook them for a few moments in half the butter. Mix with the vermicelli. Put in the bottom of a buttered soufflé dish. Make a sauce with the remaining butter, the flour, and the heated milk. Stir in the grated cheese and season well with sea salt and black pepper. Add the beaten egg yolks off the heat. Beat the egg whites until stiff and fold in. Pour half the soufflé mixture over the vermicelli and mix lightly. Pour the rest on top and sprinkle with paprika. Cook for 25 minutes at 350°. Slightly more substantial than the usual soufflé, this makes a first course for 5–6, or a light main course for 4, with a green salad.

FISH

CURRIED FISH
FISH PUDDING
RAIE AU BEURRE NOIR (SKATE)
SMOKED HADDOCK MONTE CARLO
SMOKED HADDOCK MORNAY
SMOKED HADDOCK MOUSSE
TURBOT (OR HALIBUT) GRATIN

CHRISTMAS PIE

First, bone a fowl, a wild duck, a pheasant, and two woodcocks, etc.; having spread them open on the table, season them with aromatic herbs; pepper and salt; garnish each with some forcemeat; sew them up with small twine; place them on a pan with a little clarified butter, and set them to bake in a moderate heat until they are done through, when they must be withdrawn from the oven, and put in the cool. Meanwhile, place the carcases in a stewpan, with two calf's feet, carrots, celery, onion, a clove of garlic, two bayleaves, thyme, cloves, mace and a little salt; fill up with four quarts of water; boil, skim, and then set this by the side to continue gently boiling for three hours, when it must be strained, freed from grease, boiled down to thin glaze, and kept in reserve.

Make four pounds of hot-water paste, and use this to line a raised pie-mould; line the inside of the pie with some of the forcemeat; arrange the baked fowl, duck, etc. in the centre with layers of forcemeat and seasoning, until all the preparation is used up; put a cover of paste on the top; weld it all round; cut the edge even; pinch it with pastry-pincers; ornament the top with leaves of paste; egg it over and bake the pie for about two hours and a half. When it comes out of the oven, pour in the game-glaze through a funnel; put it in the larder to get cold. Previously to sending it to table, remove the lid, garnish the top with aspic jelly; place the pie on a napkin in its dish and ornament the base with a border of freshly picked parsley.

Note.—The addition of truffles would be an improvement.

FRANCATELLI'S COOK'S GUIDE, London, 1884

CURRIED FISH

1 leek
1 carrot
1 stalk celery
3 stalks parsley
½ bay leaf

curry sauce:
1½ oz butter
2 onions
2 cloves garlic (optional)
1 Tbs light curry powder (Spice Islands or Sea Isle)
¼ tsp ground turmeric
¼ tsp ground cummin
¼ tsp ground coriander

6 black peppercorns
1 tsp sea salt
1½ lb fresh haddock fillet
3 Tbs desiccated coconut (or ground almonds)

⅛ tsp ground chilli
2 oz ground almonds
1 lime, or ½ lemon
1 Tbs crab apple (or red currant) jelly
½ gill yoghurt
2 Tbs slivered almonds

Slice the vegetables and simmer for 30 minutes in water with salt and peppercorns. Add the fish, cut in large pieces, and poach for about 12 minutes. Remove the fish and boil up the liquid until well flavoured. You will need 1 pint. Put the desiccated coconut (ground almonds can be used but they are much more expensive) in a jug and pour over ½ pint of the boiling fish stock. Leave for 20–30 minutes. Flake the fish, removing skin and bone. Make the sauce: melt the butter and cook the finely sliced onions gently until golden, adding the minced garlic, if used, towards the end. Stir in the curry powder and spices and cook for 4 minutes. Add the almonds and cook for another 2–3 minutes. Pour on the remaining ½ pint fish stock and simmer for 15 minutes. Stir in the lime (or lemon) juice, the fruit jelly, and the coconut milk which you have poured through a strainer and squeezed lightly with the back of a wooden spoon. When all is blended, taste for seasoning, add the yoghurt and do not allow to boil again. Add the fish and re-heat gently. Pour into a serving dish, scatter the almonds over the top, and serve with a dish of boiled rice. An excellent light curry, this is even better when made a few hours in advance and re-heated; it is also delicious cold.

FISH PUDDING

1½ lb fresh haddock (or cod) fillet
4 oz fresh white breadcrumbs
¼ pt milk
1½ oz butter
¼ lb mushrooms, or 2 Tbs finely
   chopped parsley

3 eggs
sea salt and black pepper
tomato sauce (page 87), or spinach
   sauce (page 86)

Chop the raw fish, discarding the skin, and pound in a mortar. Soak the breadcrumbs in the milk for 5 minutes. Cut the butter in small pieces and add to the fish in the mortar. Pound again until a smooth paste. Squeeze out excess milk from the crumbs and add them to the fish. Pound all together until smooth and amalgamated. Chop the mushrooms finely and stir into the mixture (alternatively, stir in the chopped parsley). Season with sea salt and black pepper. Beat the eggs and stir in. Pour the mixture into a buttered mould or soufflé dish, or into small moulds, allowing one for each person (large oeuf en cocotte' dishes do very well). Bake in a low oven, 325°, allowing 50 minutes for a large dish or 30 minutes for individual dishes. Serve with tomato sauce (page 87). Alternatively, make a smoother mixture by blending the raw fish with the butter and breadcrumbs in the liquidiser in small batches, instead of pounding. Stir in the mushrooms or the parsley after removing from the liquidiser. Cook by steaming rather than baking, allowing 1½ hours in a buttered pudding basin, with boiling water coming half-way up it, in a covered saucepan. Turn out to serve, and accompany with a spinach sauce. This makes a fairly small dish, but it is quite substantial and will serve 5 or 6 as a first course, or 4 as a main course. No vegetables are needed, except possibly a green salad.

RAIE AU BEURRE NOIR

3 lb skate, skinned by the fish-
   monger
1 onion
1 bay leaf
a small bunch of parsley

¼ cup white wine vinegar
1 Tbs drained capers
4 oz butter
3 Tbs white wine vinegar

Put the quartered onion, the bay leaf, and the parsley stalks in a broad pan with the vinegar and enough cold water to cover the fish. Bring to the boil and simmer for 30 minutes. Put in the skate, bring back to the boil, and simmer gently for 20 minutes. Lift out the fish and remove the bones. Lay on a large flat dish and sprinkle with the chopped parsley – about 2 tablespoonfuls – and the capers. Heat the butter slowly until dark brown and pour over the fish. Heat the vinegar and pour over all. Serves 6.

SMOKED HADDOCK MONTE CARLO

3 smoked haddocks	6 eggs
½ pt milk	¼ pt cream
1 lb tomatoes	sea salt and black pepper
2 oz butter	

Cut the haddocks in half and lay in a large shallow pan. Pour over the milk, then add enough water to barely cover them. Bring to the boil and simmer gently for 12 minutes. Lift out the haddocks and keep warm. Boil up the cooking liquor until reduced and well-flavoured. Peel the tomatoes and chop them coarsely. Melt the butter in a sauté pan and cook the tomatoes in it for about 5 minutes, till softened. Boil the eggs for 5 minutes exactly, then shell them carefully under a gently running cold tap. Put the tomatoes in a shallow gratin dish, lay the haddock pieces on top, and put an egg on top of each one. Heat the cream in a small pan with an equal amount of the reduced cooking liquor, season well with sea salt (not too much), and black pepper. When very hot, pour over the dish and serve. This makes an excellent light meal, accompanied by a lettuce salad.

SMOKED HADDOCK MORNAY

3 large smoked haddocks	black pepper
2 oz butter	½ pt thin cream
1½ Tbs flour	3 oz grated Parmesan
½ pt milk	3 oz grated Gruyère

Cut the haddocks in large pieces and put them in a pan. Pour over the milk and add enough water to just cover them. Bring to the boil and simmer for 12 minutes. Lift out the fish and cool slightly while continuing to boil up the cooking liquor to reduce it a little. Flake the fish into a bowl and keep warm while making the sauce. Melt the butter, stir in the flour and cook for 2–3 minutes. Measure $\frac{3}{4}$ pt of the cooking liquor and blend with the roux. Stir in the cream and season with black pepper. Add the cheese – the mixture of cheeses gives an excellent flavour, but is not, of course, essential. When it is smooth, mix about three-quarters of it with the haddock and pour into a gratin dish. Pour the remaining sauce over the top and scatter the reserved cheese over it. Brown quickly under the grill, re-heating the fish at the same time. Alternatively, prepare in advance and re-heat for 30 minutes in the oven at 350°, finishing off under the grill if it is not sufficiently browned. Serve with a lettuce salad as a main course or alone as a quite substantial first course.

SMOKED HADDOCK MOUSSE

2 large smoked haddocks	6 peppercorns
1 carrot	salt
1 onion	1 lemon
1 leek	$\frac{1}{2}$ oz gelatine
3 stalks parsley	$\frac{1}{2}$ pt thick cream
1 bay leaf	cayenne pepper

Put the sliced carrot, onion and leek in cold water in a fairly large pan with the peppercorns and some salt, the parsley and bay leaf, and bring to the boil. Simmer for 30 minutes. Cut the haddocks in quarters and poach in the court bouillon for 12 minutes. Lift out the fish and drain. Continue to boil up the court bouillon until well flavoured and reduced, without allowing it to become too salty. Take $\frac{1}{2}$ gill of it and dissolve the gelatine in it. Flake the fish, discarding all skin and bone, and weigh it. You should have about 1 lb. Put it in the blender with $1\frac{1}{2}$ gills of the reduced court-bouillon. Blend till smooth, adding 2 Tbs lemon juice, cayenne pepper, and extra salt if required. Stir in the dissolved gelatine. Beat the cream and fold in. Pour into a soufflé dish and chill in the refrigerator.

TURBOT (OR HALIBUT) GRATIN

2 lb turbot or halibut
$\frac{1}{4}$ pt white wine
$\frac{1}{2}$ onion
1 bay leaf
1 carrot
1 stalk celery
1 tsp sea salt

6 black peppercorns
2 oz butter
2 Tbs flour
$\frac{1}{2}$ pt thin cream
2 Tbs finely chopped parsley
   (optional)

Put enough cold water to cover the fish in a large shallow pan or fish kettle. Do not put in the fish yet. Add the flavouring vegetables and herbs, the salt and pepper. Add the wine, (if there is none readily available, you can substitute 2 Tbs white wine vinegar) and bring slowly to the boil. Simmer for 30 minutes to flavour the court bouillon, then put in the fish. Poach very gently for about 20 minutes, or till it flakes easily with a fork. Lift out the fish and boil up the stock to reduce and concentrate the flavour. Be careful it does not get too salty. When the fish is cool enough to handle, remove the skin and bone and break into pieces, or large flakes. Melt the butter, stir in the flour, and cook for a minute or two. Strain $\frac{1}{2}$ pint of the court-bouillon and blend with the roux. Add the cream and taste for seasoning. Mix lightly with the fish and pour into a shallow gratin dish. Either serve immediately, sprinkled with 2 Tbs finely chopped parsley, or put in the oven for 10 minutes at 400° to brown slightly.

A simpler version of this dish, but still good, can be made with cod or haddock fillet, and a mixture of milk and water instead of the court bouillon.

POULTRY AND GAME

ROAST CAPON
CHAUDFROID OF CHICKEN
PINK CHICKEN CASSEROLE
FRIED CHICKEN
CHICKEN PIE
GUINEA FOWL A LA VIENNOISE
BONED GOOSE
ROAST GOOSE
ROAST TURKEY I
ROAST TURKEY II

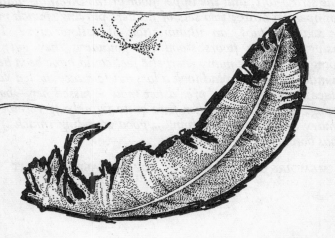

The great event of the Christmas time was the Floaters' ball. As the harvest-home belonged to the farm, this entertainment was given to the forest – all engaged in wood manufacture, their wives and families, being invited. The amusements began pretty early in the day with a game of 'ba', the hockey of the low country, our Scotch substitute for cricket. It is played on a field by two parties, who toss a small ball between them by means of crooked sticks called clubs. The Highlanders are extremely fond of this exciting game, and continue it for hours on a holiday, exhibiting during its progress many feats of agility. There were always crowds of spectators. Our people kept up the game till dark, when all the men – above a hundred – went to dinner in the barn, a cow and some sheep having been killed for them. The kitchens of both house and farm had been busy for a couple of days cooking for the entertainment. The women, as they arrived, were taken into the grieve's house for tea, a delicate attention, fully appreciated.

We delighted in the Floaters' ball, so large a party, so many strangers, some splendid dancers from Strathspey, the hay-loft, the straw-loft, and the upper floor of the threshing-mill all thrown open en suite; *two sets of fiddlers playing, punch made in the washing-tubs, an illumination of tallow dips! It is surprising that the floors stood the pounding they got; the thumping noise of the many energetic feet could have been heard half a mile off. When a lad took a lass out to dance, he led her to her place in the reel and 'pree'd her mou' – kissed her – before beginning, she holding up her face quite frankly to receive the customary salute, and he giving a good sounding smack if the lass was bonnie.*

MEMOIRS OF A HIGHLAND LADY, ELIZABETH GRANT
OF ROTHIEMURCHUS, 1898

ROAST CAPON

For a small party, a capon can well be substituted for the more traditional turkey. These giant chickens, weighing 5–6 lb when prepared for the oven, are very tender and if stuffed and carefully cooked can make a most impressive and delicious meal. I usually treat a capon in the same way as the turkey, seasoning it inside and out, then stuffing the cavity with a bread or celery and bread stuffing and wrapping it in well-buttered foil. I roast it at 350° allowing 20 minutes per lb, turning from one side to the other, then unwrapping the foil and turning it right side up for the last $\frac{1}{2}$ hour. At this stage I often add a glass of white wine to the buttery juices, and baste the capon frequently while it is browning. An excellent gravy can be made in the same way as giblet gravy, leaving aside the liver.

CHAUDFROID OF CHICKEN

2 medium sized chickens
1 onion
2 carrots
1 leek
2 stalks celery
$\frac{1}{2}$ bay leaf

3 stalks parsley
1 bunch tarragon (when available)
sea salt and black pepper
$\frac{1}{2}$ packet ($\frac{1}{4}$ oz) gelatine
$\frac{1}{2}$ pt thick cream

Poach the chickens with the onion, carrots, leek, celery, bay leaf and parsley. Add $\frac{1}{2}$ Tbs sea salt and 8 black peppercorns. When the birds are tender, after about 1 hour, remove them and strain the stock. The next day, remove all fat from the surface of the stock and boil up with the tarragon, reserving 8–10 leaves for the garnish, till it is reduced to $\frac{1}{2}$ pint, tasting for flavouring. Add more salt and pepper if necessary. Strain and dissolve the gelatine in it. Stir over ice until cool and almost setting, then whip the cream very lightly, till only half thickened, and stir in. Continue to stir over ice until very nearly set. Carve the chickens, removing the skin and dividing into neat serving pieces. Lay the pieces on a flat dish and spoon the semi-set sauce over each piece, smoothing with a palette knife.

Put in the refrigerator for $\frac{1}{2}$ hour, then spoon another layer of sauce over each piece. Decorate each piece with a tarragon leaf, and trim the edges carefully. Serve on a large flat platter. Serves 6–8.

PINK CHICKEN CASSEROLE

I large roasting chicken
I carrot
I onion
2 stalks celery
I leek
2 stalks parsley

$\frac{1}{2}$ bay leaf
$\frac{1}{2}$ Tbs sea salt
8 black peppercorns
$\frac{1}{2}$ lb noodles
6 oz mushrooms
I oz butter

sauce:
4 ripe tomatoes
$1\frac{1}{2}$ oz butter

2 Tbs flour
$\frac{1}{4}$ pt thin cream

Poach the chicken with the carrot, onion, celery, leek, parsley, bay leaf, salt and peppercorns. When it is tender, after about 1 hour, remove it and strain the stock. This can be done in advance, or indeed the whole dish can be made in advance and re-heated. Cook the noodles and make a layer of them in the bottom of a deep dish. Toss the sliced mushrooms in butter till softened and lay over the noodles. Cut the chicken into neat pieces, removing all skin and bone and lay on top of the mushrooms. Make the sauce. Skin the tomatoes and purée in the blender. Melt the butter, blend with the flour and simmer for 1 minute, stirring continuously. Pour in $\frac{1}{2}$ pt of the re-heated stock and stir till smooth. Add the cream and simmer for 4 minutes, stirring now and then. Pour in the puréed tomatoes, season to taste with sea salt and black pepper, pour over the chicken and put in a moderate oven – 350° – for 20 minutes to re-heat. If made in advance, allow 40 minutes in the oven.

FRIED CHICKEN

1 medium sized roasting chicken,
   jointed in 8 pieces
2 eggs
flour

salt and pepper
dry white breadcrumbs
nut oil

Dip the skinned pieces of chicken in seasoned flour, then in beaten egg, then in the breadcrumbs. Leave for about 30 minutes. Heat some oil in a sauté pan; you will need it about 1 inch deep. When very hot but not yet smoking, put in the pieces of chicken and turn about until brown on all sides. Pour off most of the oil and lower the heat. Cover the pan and cook gently for about 35 minutes, turning the pieces occasionally.

CHICKEN PIE

1 roasting chicken, jointed
1 onion
1 carrot
1 stalk celery
1 dessertspoon sea salt
black pepper
1½ oz butter

2 Tbs flour
½ pt thin cream
2 Tbs finely chopped parsley
¾ lb short pastry, home-made or
frozen
1 egg yolk

Put the chicken pieces in a casserole with the sliced onion, carrot, celery, sea salt and some coarsely ground black pepper. Add water to cover, bring to the boil, and simmer for 1 hour, or until chicken is tender. Lift out the chicken pieces and arrange them in a pie dish. Boil up the stock to reduce it somewhat, then strain it. Measure ¾ pint of it. Melt the butter, stir in the flour and blend. Pour on the strained stock, and add the cream. Simmer for 3 or 4 minutes, and season with salt and pepper if necessary. Stir in the chopped parsley and pour over the chicken pieces in the pie dish. Cover with pastry, brush with egg yolk and bake for 20 minutes at 400°, until crust is golden. If preferred, the chicken can be cut off the bone. In this case a large chicken can be used as the pie becomes more densely packed, and will consequently feed more people.

GUINEA FOWL A LA VIENNOISE

2 carrots
1 onion
2 stalks celery
1 bay leaf
parsley
sea salt and black pepper

$\frac{1}{4}$ pt red wine vinegar
$\frac{1}{4}$ pt water
2 guinea fowl
6 rashers thin green bacon
2 tsp flour
$\frac{1}{2}$ pt sour cream

Cut the carrots, the onion and the celery in slices. Put in a small bowl with the bay leaf and parsley, some sea salt and black pepper. Bring the vinegar and the water to the boil in a small pan and pour over the vegetables. When they are cool, pour over the birds and leave overnight. The next day, wipe the birds and tie the bacon loosely over them. Put them in a baking tin and pour the marinade with the vegetables over them. Cover with a piece of foil and cook for about 1 hour at 375°, basting often with the marinade. When the birds are tender, carve them and lay on a warm dish. Keep hot while you make the sauce. Push the vegetables and the liquid through the medium mesh of the vegetable mill, (or put through the blender for a smoother texture), then pour into a saucepan. Re-heat gently, while you mix the flour with the sour cream. When the sauce is almost boiling, stir in the cream by degrees, stirring all the time till smooth, hot, and slightly thickened. Pour over the birds, sprinkle with very finely chopped parsley, and serve with mashed potatoes or rice, and a green vegetable or a green salad. Serves 6.

BONED GOOSE

Last year, a friend who is a restaurateur gave me a boned goose as a present at Christmas time. These are not often seen, but I will include the recipe I devised to cook it in case it is of interest.

1 goose, boned
potato stuffing (see page 83)
15 juniper berries

2 Tbs olive oil
1 Tbs sea salt

Make the stuffing according to the instructions on page 83. Stuff the goose and tie up or sew, securing with skewers and fine string. Make it into as compact a parcel as possible, roughly rectangular in shape. Rub the outside of the bird with olive oil and coat with crushed sea salt and juniper berries, lightly pounded in a mortar. Lay on a rack in a roasting tin and cook for 2¼ hours in a moderate oven, 350°. Do not baste. To serve, cut across in slices and accompany with red cabbage, apple sauce or fried apple rings. Serves 8.

ROAST GOOSE

Many people prefer to cook a goose rather than a turkey for their Christmas meal, one advantage being the valuable bonus of excellent fat which it yields, while the liver is also considered a great delicacy. It must be remembered, however, that there is not nearly so much flesh on a goose as on a turkey or capon; like the duck, it has a shallow breast in relation to its size. An average goose weighs about 13 lb, (approximately 11 lb when ready for the oven), and will feed 6 people at the most, compared to a turkey of similar size which will feed 8–10 with ease.

The goose is a very fat bird, and should be treated more like a duck than a turkey. It is best stuffed with a potato stuffing (see page 83), as the blandness of the stuffing contrasts well with the fatty flesh of the bird. Prick the skin all over with a sharp fork or skewer and lay upside down on a rack in a roasting tin. Cook for the first 20 minutes at 400°, then turn the oven down to 350°, allowing 25 minutes per lb in all. (If you have the patience, it is a good idea to cook for the first 20 minutes without stuffing, then to stuff it and return it to the oven to finish cooking at the lower temperature.) Make giblet gravy in the same way as for a turkey, only adding the pan juices, free from all fat, at the end. No extra fat is needed; on the contrary, its own fat may need to be poured away once or twice during cooking. Turn right way up for the last ½ hour, but do not baste. The liver should be cooked separately, and the fat kept carefully; it is excellent for frying potatoes. Serve with apple sauce.

ROAST TURKEY I

Few people nowadays buy the mammoth birds we read about in old accounts of Christmas; I always ask for a small bird, and find a bird weighing 10–12 lb (after drawing) is a perfect size for a small party of six or seven people. Last year we were six, and a 10 lb bird was ideal. On Christmas Day itself, we only ate one side of the bird, leaving a whole side of the carcase intact to eat cold the following day. This is the best way of keeping it moist, otherwise it should be wrapped in foil or cling-wrap, for turkey is a bird that tends to dryness.

Remove the giblets, liver, etc., sprinkle the inside of the bird with salt and pepper and stuff. The gullet also should be stuffed, either with the same mixture, or with another. It only needs a small amount to fill it. It is best to sew up the bird after stuffing it, but I usually put a small peeled onion in the mouth of the cavity, and tie the legs tightly round it. The whole surface of the bird should then be generously rubbed with butter, and sprinkled with salt and pepper. Wrap a buttered sheet of aluminium foil around the bird, so that it is completely enclosed. Ideally it should then be laid on a rack in a roasting tin, but if you have no rack this is not vital. The oven should be heated to 350° and the bird should start cooking on its side. The time should be calculated, allowing 20 minutes per lb. If, like me, you prefer to keep the bird slightly underdone, so that the breast is perfectly cooked and the legs still tinged with pink, take about 10 minutes off the whole time. The advantage of this method is that you eat the white meat at its very best, while the dark meat can be re-cooked for another dish. In all, the bird will take about 3½ hours. It should be turned on its other side after 1½ hours, then turned right way up and unwrapped for the last ½ hour to brown. During this time it should be basted frequently. A bird weighing over 15 lb should be cooked in a lower oven, at 325°, allowing 15 minutes per lb.

ROAST TURKEY II

Some people disapprove of wrapping the bird in foil, saying quite rightly that this is baking rather than roasting in its true sense. They may prefer to cook it in the following way.

Lay the bird upright on a rack in a roasting tin, and have a piece of linen dipped in melted butter and laid over the breast. Cook for 25 minutes per lb at 350°, removing the cloth and basting frequently during the last $\frac{1}{2}$ hour. I have used both these methods with success, but as I only cook a turkey once a year it is hard to compare them with any great degree of accuracy.

MEAT

BEEF STEWED IN CIDER
BLANQUETTE DE VEAU
GOULASCH
BOILED HAM (OR GAMMON)
BAKED GLAZED HAM
HAM MOUSSE
HAM AND EGG RISSOLES
JAMBON PERSILLE
ROAST LOIN OF PORK
GRILLED LAMB STEAKS
NAVARIN OF LAMB
LAMB IN PASTRY
POACHED CALF'S LIVER
MEAT PIE
SMALL MUTTON PIES
STUFFED ONIONS
PORK FILLETS IN TOMATO SAUCE
ESCALOPES OF VEAL WITH MUSHROOMS
VEAL CAKES
ROAST VEAL

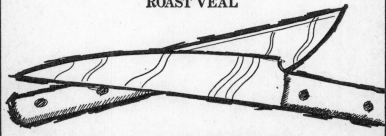

CHRISTMAS DAY IN THE WORKHOUSE

It is Christmas Day in the Workhouse,
and the cold bare walls are bright
with garlands of green and holly,
and the place is a pleasant sight:
for with clean-washed hands and faces,
in a long and hungry line
the paupers sit at their tables,
for this is the hour they dine.

And the guardians and their ladies,
although the wind is east,
have come in their furs and wrappers,
to watch their charges feast;
to smile and be condescending,
put pudding on pauper plates,
to be hosts at the workhouse banquet
they've paid for — with the rates.

BEEF STEWED IN CIDER

2 lb leg of beef
flour
salt and pepper
2 large onions
2 oz beef dripping, or oil and butter
    mixed

$\frac{3}{4}$ lb carrots
$\frac{1}{2}$ pt beef stock
$\frac{1}{2}$ pt cider
2 Tbs cider apple vinegar (from
    health food shops)
1 bay leaf

Cut the beef in neat cubes and toss in seasoned flour. Slice the onions. Melt the dripping, or the oil and butter, in a heavy casserole, and when it is hot put in the sliced onions. Stir around and leave over gentle heat to soften and become faintly coloured. Then add the meat dredged with seasoned flour, and stir around until browned on all sides. Add the carrots cut in slices. Pour on the heated stock and the cider; stir till blended. Add the vinegar, (if you have no cider apple vinegar, red wine vinegar can be used instead), and a bay leaf. Bring to boiling point and remove any scum that appears on the surface. Cover the casserole and simmer on top of the stove or in the oven for 3 hours. Taste for seasoning before serving. Serves 4–5. (For 6 people, add an extra $\frac{1}{2}$ lb beef.) Accompany with haricot beans in garlic butter and a green salad. An unusually good dish, rich and full of flavour, yet made without wine.

BLANQUETTE DE VEAU

$2\frac{1}{2}$ lb boneless veal, e.g. shoulder
$2\frac{1}{2}$ pts stock, chicken, veal or
    vegetable
1 onion stuck with 2 cloves
1 large carrot
1 bay leaf
2 stalks celery
4 stalks parsley
$\frac{3}{4}$ lb small onions

$\frac{1}{2}$ lb button mushrooms
4 oz butter
4 Tbs flour
3 egg yolks
$\frac{1}{4}$ pt thick cream
2 Tbs lemon juice
sea salt and black pepper
2–3 Tbs chopped parsley

Cut the veal in small neat pieces, about 1 inch square. Put in a casserole and cover with cold water. Bring to the boil and keep there for 2–3 minutes, then pour through a colander and rinse the meat well under the cold tap.

Return the meat to the cleaned pan and add the onion, carrot, celery, bay leaf, and parsley. Cover with the heated stock, (use a chicken stock-cube at half the usual strength if no stock is available) and bring to simmering point. Cover the pan and cook gently for $1\frac{1}{4}$ hours. Then remove the flavouring vegetables and herbs and put in the peeled onions, (if bigger than a walnut they should be parboiled for ten minutes before adding). Toss the mushrooms for a few moments in half the butter and add to the onions after 5 minutes simmering. Simmer another 5 minutes, then stir in the remaining butter and flour mixed to a paste in a cup. Stir until blended, then simmer a further 10 minutes. Beat the egg yolks in a small bowl, mix with the cream, and stir in some of the simmering veal stock. Return to the pan and stir over very gentle heat until all is blended and smooth, without allowing it to boil again. Add the lemon juice, salt and pepper to taste, sprinkle with the chopped parsley, and serve. Accompany with boiled rice and carrots, or noodles and a green salad. This is a truly excellent dish, but it is quite a lot of trouble, particularly towards the end. If serving a dessert afterwards, choose something very simple, without cream – a jelly or a compôte of fruit would be ideal. In summer time, this dish can be much improved by adding a few sprigs of fresh tarragon at the same time as the onions. Remove before serving.

GOULASCH

2 lb best stewing steak
2 onions
2 cloves garlic
1 oz butter
1 Tbs olive oil
1 Tbs flour
1 dessertspoon paprika

2 green peppers
1 lb tomatoes
$\frac{1}{4}$ pt V8 vegetable juice, tomato juice, or stock
$\frac{1}{2}$ pt sour cream
salt and pepper

Cut the meat in cubes. Chop the onion and crush the garlic. Heat the butter and oil in a casserole and cook the onion till pale golden. Add the garlic and cook a few minutes longer. Add the meat and stir around until lightly browned on all sides. Stir in the flour and add the paprika. Add the tomatoes, peeled and roughly chopped – if they are dry you may need to add $\frac{1}{4}$ pt V8, tomato juice, or stock. Cover and cook gently for 2 hours. Add the peppers cut in strips and cook for another 30 minutes. Stir in the sour cream, season and serve. Accompany with a dish of boiled rice.

BOILED HAM (OR GAMMON)

1 small ham or ½ a large ham or gammon weighing 8–10 lb	2 parsnips
3 large onions	4 stalks parsley
4 stalks celery	2 bay leaves
3 large carrots	15 peppercorns
2 turnips	½ pt cider vinegar
	½ pt sugar
	1 cup brown breadcrumbs

Scrub the ham and soak in cold water for 24 hours. Scrub the vegetables (do not peel them) and cut in equal-sized pieces. Lay them in a thick layer in a large pan and put the ham on top. Add the bay leaves and peppercorns, the parsley stalks, vinegar and sugar. Cover the ham with cold water and bring almost to boiling point. Time the cooking from the first moment bubbles start to reach the surface. Do not ever allow it to reach simmering, far less boiling. Skim off brown froth that rises to the surface. Allow 20 minutes per lb, plus 20 minutes, keeping the heat well below boiling point all the time. When the cooking time is up, turn off the heat and leave to cool in the liquid, first pouring in a cupful of cold water to arrest the cooking. When cool, lift the ham out of the water and remove the skin. Press freshly made brown breadcrumbs all over the fatty surface. (If intending to bake the ham, allow 20 minutes less cooking time. See recipe below.)

BAKED GLAZED HAM

1 boiled ham or gammon (see above)	½ cup fresh brown breadcrumbs
	1 dessertspoon French mustard
1 cup soft brown sugar	1 Tbs cider vinegar

Cook for the shorter time as indicated in the recipe. Leave ham to partially cool in the liquid then lift out and remove the skin. Mix the sugar and breadcrumbs to a paste with the mustard and vinegar. Smooth the mixture all over the fatty surface of the ham with a palette knife, pressing well in. Do not do this too far in advance of the baking or most of it will slide off. Bake for 45 minutes at 350°, basting half-way through with a little extra vinegar. Leave for 15 minutes in the oven with the heat turned off and the door slightly open, or in a warm place before attempting to carve. Serve with Cumberland sauce, or mustard sauce, or raisin sauce.

HAM MOUSSE

1½ lb ham, lean parts only
½ pt well-flavoured chicken or veal stock
½ oz (1 packet) gelatine

½ pt (¼ bottle) dry champagne or sparkling white wine
black pepper
⅓ pt thick cream
2 egg whites

Put the ham twice through the finest blade of the mincer. Heat the stock and dissolve the gelatine in it. Put it in the blender with the ham, in batches. When all is reduced to a smooth paste, turn into a large bowl and place over ice. Beat hard with a wooden spoon and add the champagne and plenty of freshly ground black pepper. When quite cool, whip the cream and fold in. Beat the egg whites until stiff and fold in also. Spoon into a soufflé dish to set. To make it look really elegant, choose a dish slightly too small to hold the mixture and tie a strip of greased foil around the rim, securing with tape. Before serving, remove the foil to give the impression of a soufflé that has risen above the edges of the dish. Alternatively, the mousse can be turned out, and garnished as you like. In summer, my favourite garnish is simply a few feathery sprigs of dill, laid in the centre of the mousse, and then half covered with a thin layer of home-made aspic jelly. But on the whole I prefer to leave well alone, rather than fooling around with garnishes. A well-made dish should look quite good enough to eat without extra decoration.

I made this once with champagne and it was delicious; I'm not sure why but it really does make a difference.

HAM AND EGG RISSOLES

1 medium onion
1½ oz butter
2 Tbs flour
¼ pt milk
3 Tbs chopped parsley
black pepper

½ lb minced ham
4 hard-boiled eggs
1 raw egg
fine breadcrumbs
butter and oil

Chop the onion and cook in the butter until golden. Add the flour, blend, and pour on the heated milk. Cook for a few moments, then stir in the chopped parsley and season with black pepper. Remove from the fire and stir in the minced ham and the chopped hard-boiled eggs. Taste for seasoning, adding more pepper if necessary, but probably no salt on account of the ham. Pour into a shallow dish and leave to cool, then chill in the refrigerator for a few hours, or overnight. This will make it easier to handle. Later, it can be formed into small flat cakes using two spoons, and laid on a floured board. Dip in raw egg beaten with 1 Tbs of top of the milk, then in fine breadcrumbs, and fry in a mixture of butter and oil. Makes eight small cakes, serves 3–4. Serve with tomato sauce and a green vegetable.

JAMBON PERSILLE

½ ham or gammon, about 6 lb
1 lb knuckle of veal
4 calves' feet, or pigs' feet if
   calves' feet are unobtainable
1 bay leaf
2 stalks parsley
1 stalk celery

10 shallots, or 6 small onions
12 black peppercorns
2 cloves
2 bottles dry white wine
3 Tbs white wine vinegar
4 Tbs chopped parsley

Soak the ham or gammon for 24 hours, changing the water two or three times. Put in a large pot and cover with fresh cold water. Bring to the boil and simmer for 30 minutes. Leave it to cool, then cut out the bone. Reserve the water. Blanch (in a similar fashion) the knuckle of veal and the calves' (or pigs') feet, but only for 10 minutes. Drain and rinse well under running water. Clean the large pot and put in the ham, veal, and feet, the herbs, shallots, cloves and peppercorns – no salt is needed. Pour over the white wine, add enough of the reserved blanching water (from the ham if it is not too salty, otherwise from the veal etc.) to cover the meat. Bring to the boil, removing all scum with a slotted spoon as it rises to the surface, and simmer very gently with the lid on for 3 hours. Take out the ham, throw away the veal, calves' feet and the flavouring vegetables and herbs, and strain the liquid. Cut the ham in fairly large pieces, about 1–2 inch cubes, and crush slightly with a fork. Press the pieces into a round bowl like a shallow pudding basin, mixing the fat and lean evenly, and after straining the liquid through a double muslin and removing all the fat, pour it over the ham, making sure that it penetrates all through the pieces and reaches the bottom of the bowl. Leave to cool overnight, in the refrigerator or a cool larder. To serve: turn out onto a flat platter and cut in slices. Serves 12.

A pretty green dish, a change from the more usual ham mousse. A very useful dish for a holiday, as it can be made several days in advance, and keeps well.

ROAST LOIN OF PORK

1 loin of pork weighing about 3½ lb   a little nut, sunflower seed, or corn oil
sea salt

Ask the butcher to cut through the chine bone for you to facilitate carving, and to score the rind. Rub the skin with oil and scatter sea salt all over it. Roast for 30 minutes per lb, starting off at 450°, then turning the oven down to 400° after 1 hour, or roughly half-way through. Remove the crackling before carving into chops, then serve a piece with each one. Serve with a purée of potatoes and chopped cabbage, and apple sauce, or mustard sauce.

GRILLED LAMB STEAKS

1 small leg of lamb, boned

garlic (or parsley) butter:
¼ lb butter
2 cloves garlic or 4 Tbs finely
   chopped parsley

sea salt and black pepper
½ lemon

Cut the boned leg of lamb across with a carving knife in 6 slices, each about
¾ inch thick. (If you have a small saw, or an obliging butcher, you could
leave the bone in.) Brush with melted butter or oil and cook under the grill
like a steak, 4–5 minutes on each side will probably be long enough. Have
the butter prepared beforehand: pound it in a mortar, beat in the crushed
garlic or the chopped parsley, and add sea salt, freshly ground black pepper
and lemon juice to taste. Chill, form into balls, and chill again. Serve the
lamb steaks on a platter with some of the butter on each one.

NAVARIN OF LAMB

approx. 2½ lb boneless lamb (a
   small leg of New Zealand lamb,
   boned, or half a larger leg)
1 oz dripping or other fat
½ pt V8 vegetable juice
½ pt beef or chicken stock
½ pt white wine (or extra stock if no
   wine available)
½ lb new potatoes
½ lb small onions

½ lb small carrots
½ lb small turnips
½ lb courgettes (if available)
½ lb string beans (if available)
½ lb frozen broad beans
¼ lb small frozen peas
4 Tbs chopped parsley
sea salt and black pepper
2 oz butter
4 Tbs flour

Cut the meat in 1 inch cubes. Melt the dripping in a casserole and brown
the meat in it. Heat the vegetable juice with the stock and wine and pour it
on. Stir till mixed and simmering, then cover and cook gently for 1 hour.
Put in the whole peeled potatoes, onions, carrots and turnips and bring
back to the boil. Cover the pan and simmer another 30 minutes. Then add
the courgettes, cut in 1-inch slices; and the beans, cut in chunks. (If these
look tough, par-boil them for 10 minutes first.) Cook another 30 minutes,

then cook the frozen vegetables briefly and add them to the casserole. Mix the butter and flour to a paste and stir into the stew. Cook gently until amalgamated and slightly thickened. Add salt and pepper to taste, sprinkle with chopped parsley, and serve. The only accompaniment needed is a loaf of fresh crusty bread to soak up the juices.

LAMB IN PASTRY

1 leg of English lamb, boned
6 Tbs chopped parsley

2 cloves garlic
sea salt and black pepper

short pastry:
12 oz flour
pinch of salt
6 oz butter

1 egg yolk
iced water

1 egg yolk

1 Tbs cream or top of the milk

Do not tie the meat, but trim off as much excess fat as possible and form into a compact shape. Weigh it and calculate the cooking time, allowing 30 minutes per lb. (It will probably weigh about 4 lb.) Heat the oven to 400° and put the meat in a baking tin. Divide the cooking time in half – for a 4 lb leg of lamb, weighed after boning, the cooking time would be 2 hours; therefore put in the oven for 1 hour, turning down the heat to 350° after ½ hour. Then remove from the oven and leave to cool for a further hour. Meanwhile, make the pastry and leave in a cool place till ready to use. When ready for the final cooking, have the oven heated to 400° and roll out the pastry thinly. Place the meat on it and scatter the chopped parsley, minced garlic, salt and pepper all over it, between it and the pastry. Wrap it round carefully, sealing the edges with water. Turn upwards and place in the cleaned baking tin. Decorate with leaves cut from the pastry trimmings, and brush all over with the egg yolk and cream mixed together. Put in the oven and cook for another hour, or whatever time you have calculated, again turning down the heat to 350° after ½ hour. Watch to make sure the pastry does not get too brown; if it shows signs of doing this, lay a piece of foil over it. When ready, it should be a beautiful golden brown. Leave for 10 minutes in a warm place before carving. Serve with home-made mint sauce, or redcurrant jelly. It is also delicious cold. Serves 8–10.

POACHED CALF'S LIVER

A friend gave me this recipe from Holland, where her husband's family cook a whole calf's liver, or a large piece, in this way every Christmas. The piece of liver is put in a large pot lying on an up-turned tin plate and covered with cold water. No seasonings or flavourings of any kind are added. The pot is covered and the water brought slowly almost to boiling point. The heat is then reduced, and the water kept just below simmering – there should not be any bubbles rising for the duration of the cooking. A piece of liver weighing between 2½–3 lb will take about 1¾ hours. Then turn off the heat and leave it to cool in its liquid. When cold, it should be lifted out very carefully, as it is extremely fragile, and put in a bowl, then covered with its liquid and put in the refrigerator. It is served very cold, sliced thinly – again, this must be done with care as it is so soft, the carver holding a piece of bread in his left hand to steady i t with – and eaten like pâté, either on bread or without, sprinkled with sea salt. The liver should be still pink inside, and tastes like an exquisite liver pâté. It is sometimes eaten on slices of fruit bread, like the Christmas bread on page 105. It will keep for several days if it is always returned to the bowl and submerged in its cooking liquid. When the liver is finished, the stock is made into soup, by making a roux with butter and flour, and blending with the heated stock. Seasonings and flavouring vegetables are added, and sometimes a small glass of port.

MEAT PIE

1 onion
½ oz beef dripping or other fat
1 carrot
1 stalk celery
1½ lb minced beef
2 tomatoes

2 Tbs chopped parsley
¼ pt stock
sea salt and black pepper
1 lb short pastry (or 1 large and 1
  small pack frozen short pastry)
1 egg yolk

Chop the onion and cook in the dripping in a frying pan. Chop the carrot and par-boil for 5 minutes in lightly salted water; drain. If you have no stock, keep the carrot water and dissolve ¼ stock cube in it. Chop the celery and add to the onion when it starts to soften. After a few minutes, add the minced beef and stir till browned. Skin and chop the tomatoes and add them to the pan. Add the drained carrot and the parsley. Moisten with the stock (or carrot water) and simmer for 5 minutes. Leave to cool. Make the pastry and divide into uneven pieces. Roll out the larger one and line a 9–10 inch flan ring. Season the meat filling well with salt and pepper and drain off the liquid, reserving it. Put the filling in the pastry case and roll out the remaining pastry to make a lid. Cover the pie and seal the edges. Make a hole in the middle, and brush with beaten egg yolk. Cook for 15 minutes at 400°, then a further 20 minutes at 350°, covering with a piece of foil if the top gets too brown. Before serving, skim the fat off the reserved stock and heat it. Either pour into the hole in the lid through a funnel, or serve separately in a sauce boat. Good served with turnips in cream (see page 79). This useful pie can also be eaten cold or re-heated.

SMALL MUTTON PIES

2 lb pastry, short, flaky or puff
2 lb minced leg of lamb, with the
  bone if possible
2 onions
2 carrots

1 stalk celery
½ bay leaf
2 Tbs chopped parsley
sea salt and black pepper
1 egg yolk

Ask the butcher to give you half a leg of lamb with the bone. In the morning, make about a pint of stock with the bone, 1 carrot, 1 onion, 1 stalk celery and half a bay leaf. (Alternatively, use beef stock or a cube.) Strain it and leave to cool. Remove the fat. Later in the day, make the meat filling. Chop the remaining onion and carrot finely and mix with the meat and the chopped parsley. Put in a pot with ¾ pint of the stock and bring to the boil. Add salt and pepper and simmer gently, stirring often, for 10 minutes. Turn into a colander over a bowl, and leave to cool. When the filling has completely cooled, roll out the pastry very thinly indeed. Line 12 small round tins with pastry, and divide the filling among them. Pour 2 Tbs of the cooking liquid into each pie and cover with a pastry lid. Brush with beaten egg yolk and make a small slit in the centre of each. Bake at 400° for 25–35 minutes, according to size, watching to make sure they do not burn. Remove from the oven and pour the remaining ¼ pt stock through a funnel into each one. (If you prefer, this can be slightly thickened first, with 1 tsp of flour mixed with 1 tsp of butter. Alternatively, it can be omitted altogether but it does stop them being dry.) Makes 12 small pies; serves 8–10 or 12 as part of a meal.

These little pies are excellent hot, cold, or re-heated. They will also keep hot for hours without spoiling. We always used to have them for picnic lunches when we lived in Scotland.

STUFFED ONIONS

6 Spanish onions
½ oz dripping
¾ lb minced beef
½ lb tomatoes
2 stalks celery (chopped)
1 clove garlic

sea salt and black pepper
2 Tbs chopped parsley
1 oz butter
1½ Tbs flour
¼ pt creamy milk, or thin cream
2 Tbs grated Parmesan or Gruyère

Put the whole onions in a large pan and cover with cold, lightly salted water. Bring to the boil and cook until they are soft when pierced with a skewer. After about 1 hour lift them out and drain them, keeping the water. When cool enough to handle, scoop out the insides leaving an outside wall to contain the stuffing. Reserve the insides for another dish. Melt ½ oz dripping or other fat in a frying pan and cook the minced beef in it until browned all over. Add the celery and garlic, then the tomatoes, peeled and finely chopped. Stir often, and cook till all is browned and softened. Season well with salt and pepper and stir in the parsley. Using a perforated spoon, stuff the onions with the mixture, leaving behind the juice. Place them in a baking dish. Make the sauce: melt the butter, stir in the flour, and pour on $\frac{1}{2}$ pt of the reserved onion water. Blend and simmer for 5 minutes, then stir in the milk or cream. Simmer another 2–3 minutes, then add the cheese. Stir till melted, adjust the seasoning, then pour the sauce over the onions. Cook for 25 minutes at 350°.

PORK FILLETS IN TOMATO SAUCE

2 pork fillets (weighing about $\frac{3}{4}$ lb each)

approx. 3 oz butter
a little olive or nut oil

tomato sauce (a):
1 small tin condensed tomato purée
$\frac{1}{2}$ pt thick cream

sea salt and black pepper
a little lemon juice

tomato sauce (b):
$\frac{1}{4}$ pt V8 vegetable juice, or tomato juice
$\frac{1}{4}$ pt sour cream

sea salt and black pepper
a little lemon juice

Trim all fat off the fillets and cut them in thin slices. Lay the little slices on a sheet of transparent cling-wrap, or cellophane paper. Lay another sheet on top of them, and beat them flat with a rolling-pin. Heat some butter and a little oil in a large frying pan, or two smaller pans, and cook the slices briskly until golden brown on both sides. Remove them to a heated dish and keep warm while you fry another batch. When all the meat is cooked, make the sauce. For sauce (a), scrape all the juices together in one pan and stir in the tomato purée. Pour in the cream, stir until well amalgamated, season with salt and pepper and a little lemon juice, and pour over the meat. For sauce (b), pour the vegetable juice into the pan and cook for a moment or two with the juices, then stir in the sour cream till well mixed. Season with salt and pepper and a few drops lemon juice, and pour over the meat. Serve with noodles or rice, and a green salad.

ESCALOPES OF VEAL WITH MUSHROOMS

6 veal escalopes
3 oz butter
½ lb flat mushrooms

½ pt sour cream
sea salt and black pepper

Cook the escalopes gently in half the butter. Slice the mushrooms and cook in the remaining butter. Add the sour cream, stir until well heated, season with salt and pepper, and pour over the veal. Serve with noodles or rice and a green salad.

VEAL CAKES

½ lb cold roast veal
1 onion
1 clove garlic
1 oz butter
2 oz soft white breadcrumbs

2 Tbs chopped parsley
1 egg
¼ pt milk (approx.)
sea salt and black pepper
butter

Mince the veal, discarding all fat. Chop the onion finely and cook till golden in the butter, adding the finely chopped garlic half-way through. Add the breadcrumbs and stir round in the butter till well mixed and slightly browned. Add the egg beaten with just enough milk to make the mixture hold together. Season well. Make into round flat cakes like small hamburgers and fry till golden brown on each side in butter. Excellent served with fried parsley (see page 78). Makes 8 cakes; serves 3–4.

ROAST VEAL

1 rolled loin of veal, 3–3½ lb
French mustard
2 oz butter

¼ pt white wine
sea salt

Sprinkle the outside of the joint with salt and rub with mustard. Put on a rack in a roasting tin with the butter and ¼ pt hot water. Roast for 40 minutes per lb at 325°, basting 2 or 3 times. Half-way through, pour a wine glass full of white wine over the meat. Continue to baste. After moving the joint to a serving dish, scrape the juices together over a flame on top of the stove, adding a little more hot water if necessary. Serve the meat with noodles and a green salad, and the gravy in a sauce boat.

VEGETABLES

BRUSSELS SPROUTS AND CHESTNUTS
CARROTS WITH SOUR CREAM
CHESTNUTS IN SAUCE
HARICOT BEANS IN GARLIC BUTTER
GRATIN OF JERUSALEM ARTICHOKES
AN EXCELLENT MIXED SALAD
FRIED PARSLEY
PARSNIP CROQUETTES
STRING BEANS AND ALMONDS
TURNIPS IN CREAM SAUCE

How did you survive Xmas? I suppose by now your digestion is properly ruined and you are filled with gloomy vapours and a dislike for the human race . . .'

LETTER TO GERALD BRENAN, 27 DECEMBER 1926
CARRINGTON, LETTERS AND EXTRACTS FROM HER DIARY,
JONATHAN CAPE, 1970

BRUSSELS SPROUTS AND CHESTNUTS

$1\frac{1}{2}$ lb small brussels sprouts
$\frac{1}{2}$ lb chestnuts

1 oz butter
sea salt and black pepper

Bake the chestnuts until the skins can be removed. Cut the nuts in halves or quarters. Boil the sprouts briskly until just tender; drain well and dry out over a gentle heat. Add the nuts and the butter cut in small pieces. Season well with sea salt and coarsely ground black pepper. Serve as soon as possible. Excellent with turkey.

CARROTS WITH SOUR CREAM

1 lb carrots
4 rashers bacon
$\frac{1}{4}$ pt sour cream

a little lemon juice
black pepper

Slice the carrots and cook in salted water till soft. Drain well. Chop the bacon and fry gently till crisp. Pour the sour cream into the pan with the bacon and stir around until hot and well mixed. Season with black pepper and a little lemon juice. Pour over the carrots and serve.

CHESTNUTS IN SAUCE

1 lb chestnuts
$\frac{3}{4}$ pt chicken stock
1 carrot
1 onion

1 oz butter
1 Tbs flour
$\frac{1}{2}$ gill cream
2 Tbs chopped parsley

Peel the chestnuts: make a small nick in each nut, using a small, sharp, strong knife to piece the shell. Put them in a pan and cover with cold water. Bring quickly to the boil, then remove from the heat. Using a slotted spoon, lift out a few nuts at a time and remove the shells, using the same small knife and your fingernails. The shells will only come away easily while the nuts are still very hot, so if they start to become difficult, re-heat the pan until boiling point is almost reached.

When all the nuts are peeled, put them in a small pan with the chicken stock. Bring to the boil and simmer gently for 7–8 minutes, by which time they will probably be tender. Drain them, reserving the stock, which should measure roughly ½ pint. Melt the butter, stir in the flour and simmer till blended, then pour on the stock. Simmer till smooth, and add the cream. Add salt and pepper to taste, and put in the chestnuts to re-heat. Stir in the chopped parsley at the last moment. This makes a small dish to serve as a side-dish, half-way between a vegetable dish and a sauce, for 5–6 people. It makes a delicious accompaniment to roast turkey, or poultry or game. It can be made in larger quantities but the initial shelling of the nuts is a lengthy business when done on a large scale. It also has the advantage of keeping well without spoiling, so it can be prepared an hour in advance of the rest of the meal when necessary.

HARICOT BEANS IN GARLIC BUTTER

½ lb haricot beans (French or
    Italian if possible)
½ onion
1 carrot
1 stalk celery
½ bay leaf

sea salt and black pepper
4 oz butter
2 cloves garlic (or 4 Tbs finely
    chopped parsley if preferred)
½ lemon

Put the beans in a saucepan, cover with cold water, and bring slowly to the boil. When the water boils, turn off the heat and cover the pan. Leave for 1 hour (or longer, as you wish). Then bring the water back to the boil, skim it, and put in the onion, carrot, celery and bay leaf. Cover again and simmer gently, adding salt after 30 minutes. The beans will probably be tender in 1 hour. Add more boiling water during the cooking if necessary. When soft but not broken up, drain off the water and keep for soup with the flavouring vegetables. Make the garlic butter while the beans are cooking: pound the butter in a mortar, or beat till smooth with a wooden spoon. Beat in the crushed garlic, (or parsley if preferred), and add lemon juice to taste and plenty of sea salt and black pepper. When the beans are ready, stir in the butter and serve. Delicious with beef stews or roast lamb.

GRATIN OF JERUSALEM ARTICHOKES

1½ lb Jerusalem artichokes (sliced)

sauce:

2 oz butter
3 Tbs flour
¼ pt milk
¼ pt thin cream

¼ lb grated Gruyère, or Gruyère
    and Parmesan mixed
sea salt and black pepper

Scrape the artichokes and throw into cold water. Salt it lightly and bring to the boil. Cook briskly until they are soft – about 20 minutes. Drain them well, reserving the water, and return to the pan to dry out a little over gentle heat. Leave in a warm place while you make the sauce. Melt the butter, stir in the flour and cook for 2 minutes. Take ½ pt of the reserved cooking water and mix with the milk. Pour it on to the roux and stir till blended. Simmer for 5 minutes, then add the cream. Simmer for another 2–3 minutes, then stir in the grated cheese (a mixture of cheeses gives an excellent flavour). Stir till smooth, then season well with salt and pepper. Put the artichokes in a shallow gratin dish and pour the sauce over them. Put in a hot oven to brown – 12–15 minutes at 400°. Alternatively, this can be prepared in advance and re-heated for 30 minutes at 350°; if the top is not sufficiently browned it can be finished off under the grill.

AN EXCELLENT MIXED SALAD

1 cucumber
1 large green pepper
2 carrots
1 apple
1 celery heart

1 heart of a cos or Webb's lettuce
2 oz pine kernels
sea salt and black pepper
sunflower-seed oil
lemon juice

Peel the cucumber and chop it finely. Chop the pepper finely, also the carrots, the unpeeled apple and the celery. Shred the lettuce. Mix all together in a large bowl and scatter in the pine kernels. Add a little salt and pepper, and some sunflower-seed oil and lemon juice, not as much as you would use for a lettuce salad, but just enough to moisten it lightly. Serve alone, or with a tomato salad and a dish of sliced feta (soft white Greek cheese) as a complete course.

FRIED PARSLEY

This is an old-fashioned garnish that is rarely seen nowadays; it makes a very pretty decoration, and is both delicious and highly nutritious. It should be served as an accompaniment to fried dishes such as croquettes and rissoles, and fried fillets of fish or shellfish.

Choose sprigs of very fresh parsley and wash and dry them well. Have a deep pan of oil heated to about 325°. Drop in the parsley, a few sprigs at a time, and cook for about 3 minutes only, turning over once. When bright emerald green lift out and drain on soft paper; it should be very crisp, almost brittle.

PARSNIP CROQUETTES

1½ lb parsnips	2 eggs
1 oz butter	2 Tbs chopped parsley
2 Tbs thick cream	fine dry breadcrumbs
sea salt and black pepper	butter and oil, or deep oil

Boil the parsnips and drain well. Dry out over gentle heat and measure the purée; you should have about 1 pint. Push through the vegetable mill and, if necessary, dry out again. It is amazing how much moisture parsnips will retain. When a reasonably dry purée is obtained, stir in the butter and cream and season with salt and pepper. Remove from the heat and stir in 1 beaten egg and the chopped parsley. Chill the mixture for some hours in the refrigerator to firm it. When ready to cook, shape into rolls or small round cakes and lay on a floured board. Dip them in the remaining egg, beaten with a drop of cream or top of the milk, then in fine crumbs to form an even coating. Sauté them in a mixture of butter and oil, turning them over to brown on both sides, or drop into a pan of deep oil heated to 360°. Serves 4–5 as an accompaniment to a main dish, or 3 as a dish on its own, with fried parsley and a tomato sauce.

STRING BEANS AND ALMONDS

1½ lb string beans	sea salt and black pepper
1 oz butter	4 oz blanched and peeled almonds

Leave the beans whole and cook them until just tender. Drain well and return to the pan. Add the butter and plenty of sea salt and black pepper. Then shake in the almonds, cut in thin slices. Stir well and serve.

TURNIPS IN CREAM SAUCE

1½ lb young turnips	6 Tbs finely chopped parsley
2 oz butter	sea salt and black pepper
¼ pt thick cream	

If the turnips are very small, leave them whole; otherwise cut them in halves or quarters. Cover them with cold water, bring to the boil and cook briskly till tender – they will take from 20 to 30 minutes, depending on size. Drain them well and return them to the pan to dry out over very gentle heat. In a small pan melt the butter and add the cream. Simmer for 2 minutes, stir in the parsley, some sea salt and black pepper and pour over the turnips in the serving dish.

STUFFINGS AND SAUCES

BREAD STUFFING
CELERY STUFFING
POTATO STUFFING
SAUSAGE MEAT STUFFING
SAUSAGE AND CHESTNUT STUFFING

APPLE SAUCE
BREAD SAUCE
CRANBERRY SAUCE
SPINACH SAUCE
TOMATO SAUCE
CUSTARD SAUCE
HOT JAM SAUCE
RAISIN SAUCE
RASPBERRY SAUCE
HOT TOFFEE SAUCE

Small boy. 'Were there any sweets ?'
Self. 'Of course there were sweets. It was the marshmallows that squelched. Hard-boileds, toffee, fudge and allsorts, crunches, cracknels, humbugs, glaciers, and marzipan and butterwelsh for the Welsh.'

CONVERSATIONS ABOUT CHRISTMAS, DYLAN THOMAS, 1955

BREAD STUFFING

¾ lb shallots (or ½ lb onions)
4 oz butter
¾ lb soft white breadcrumbs

1 cup (1½ oz) chopped parsley
sea salt and black pepper

Chop the shallots (or onions) finely and sauté in the butter until golden. Add the breadcrumbs and stir round until well mixed. Remove from the heat and stir in the chopped parsley. Season with plenty of sea salt and black pepper. Leave to cool before using. Enough to stuff a 12 lb turkey; can be made in half quantities for a large chicken.

CELERY STUFFING

1 head celery
½ lb soft white breadcrumbs
1 dessertspoon sea salt
black pepper

1 tsp black peppercorns
¼ tsp ground mace
2 eggs
2 oz butter

Discard the outer stalks of the celery and chop the inner stalks finely. Mix with the breadcrumbs in a bowl and add the sea salt and black pepper, roughly crushed in a mortar, also the mace. (If you have none, nutmeg can be used instead.) Beat the eggs and stir them into the mixture, then stir in the butter, which you have placed in a saucer over a pan of hot water till half melted. Mix well together before using to stuff a capon or small turkey.

POTATO STUFFING

2 medium onions
1 oz beef dripping, or other fat
1 lb pure pork sausage meat*
1 lb freshly mashed potatoes

1 small tin soft green peppercorns
1 Tbs sea salt
6–8 Tbs chopped parsley

Chop the onions and brown lightly in the fat. Add the sausage meat (if pure pork is not available, buy the best quality you can get) and stir around until it is lightly browned. Remove from the heat and stir in the hot mashed potatoes. Pound the green peppercorns to a paste in a mortar with the sea salt, then stir into the mixture. Add the parsley and mix well. Taste and adjust seasonings accordingly. An excellent stuffing for roast goose; also good with turkey or capon.

* Pure pork sausage meat can be bought from Harrods, and a few good shops. If not available, use the best quality sausage meat you can get, or buy good quality sausages and skin them.

SAUSAGE MEAT STUFFING

2 lb pure pork sausage meat
1 Tbs onion juice (made in a garlic press)
1 tsp sea salt
10 black peppercorns, roughly crushed

$\frac{1}{2}$ tsp mixed spice, or mixed cinnamon, mace, and cloves
1 cup (1$\frac{1}{2}$ oz) chopped parsley
1 Tbs brandy

Mix all the ingredients together and adjust seasoning to taste. This makes enough to stuff a 12 lb turkey; I usually make it in half the above quantities and use it to stuff the neck and to make little forcemeat balls, as I prefer a bread stuffing for the main body of the bird.

SAUSAGE AND CHESTNUT STUFFING

1 lb pure pork sausage meat
1 lb chestnuts
$\frac{1}{4}$ lb shallots
1 clove garlic
4 Tbs finely chopped parsley

1 Tbs brandy
1 dessertspoon sea salt
black pepper
ground mace or nutmeg
milk

Pure pork sausage meat can be bought from Harrods, but a good quality sausage will do instead. Mash the sausage meat in a deep bowl. Shell the chestnuts (see page 19) and simmer in milk for 8–10 minutes till tender. Chop them coarsely and mix with the sausage meat. Chop the shallots and garlic finely and add. Stir in the parsley, brandy, sea salt and plenty of freshly ground black pepper with a little mace or nutmeg. Try out seasoning by frying a small ball. When all is well seasoned and mixed, use to stuff a small turkey or capon. This mixture is also delicious made into small balls and fried, to serve with turkey, chicken, or game.

APPLE SAUCE

2 Bramley cooking apples	a little lemon juice
a pinch of sugar	$\frac{1}{2}$ oz butter

Peel and core the apples and slice thickly. Put in a small pan with just enough water to cover the bottom. Add a pinch of sugar and cover the pan. Bring to the boil and simmer for 8–10 minutes, stirring now and then till the slices are soft and broken up. Do not allow to stick to the bottom. Put through the coarse mesh of the vegetable mill or leave as it is; it can be made smooth by putting through a baby food strainer or in the blender, but I prefer to leave it rather lumpy. Stir in a squeeze of lemon juice and a knob of butter before serving. Serve with roast pork, duck, or goose.

BREAD SAUCE

a generous $\frac{1}{2}$ pt milk	approx. 6 Tbs fresh white
$\frac{1}{2}$ onion	breadcrumbs
2 cloves	sea salt and black pepper
$\frac{1}{2}$ bay leaf	$\frac{1}{2}$ oz butter
	2 Tbs cream

Put the milk in a small pan with the onion stuck with the cloves and the $\frac{1}{2}$ bay leaf. Bring to the boil and turn off the heat. Cover the pan and leave at the side of the stove for 20–30 minutes to infuse. When ready to make the sauce, throw away the onion, cloves and bay leaf, and bring back to simmering point. Add the crumbs gradually, stopping when the desired consistency is reached, remembering it will thicken a little during the cooking. Simmer for about 3 minutes, season carefully with sea salt and black pepper, add a small knob of butter and a little cream if you have it, and serve. Do not make long in advance as it will become thick and puddingy. When well made, this traditional English sauce can be truly delicious; serve with roast chicken, turkey, or game.

CRANBERRY SAUCE

1 lb cranberries	$\frac{1}{2}$ lb sugar
$\frac{3}{4}$ pt water	1 Tbs orange juice

Wash and pick over the cranberries. Bring the water and the sugar to the boil and add the berries. Bring back to the boil and simmer for about 3 minutes, till the berries start to burst. Turn off the heat and cover the pan. A little later, pour into a bowl and add the orange juice. Leave to cool so that the sauce will thicken somewhat. This makes a lot of sauce, about 2 pints, but it is quickly made and will keep in the refrigerator over the holiday. Alternatively, it can be made in half quantities. Serve cold, with hot or cold roast turkey, capon, ham, etc. An excellent sauce, with a tart fresh taste.

SPINACH SAUCE

a large packet ($\frac{1}{2}$ lb) frozen chopped spinach	$\frac{1}{4}$ pint milk
1 oz butter	$\frac{1}{4}$ pint thin cream
1 Tbs flour	sea salt and black pepper
	ground nutmeg

Cook the spinach according to the directions on the packet; drain well. Make a sauce with the butter, flour and heated milk. Stir in the cream and the spinach purée. Put in the blender, then pour back into the clean pan. Re-heat and add sea salt and black pepper and a pinch of ground nutmeg to taste. A good sauce to serve with the poached fish pudding on page 42.

TOMATO SAUCE

1 onion
1½ oz butter
1 clove garlic (optional)

¾ lb tomatoes
sea salt and black pepper
a pinch of sugar

Chop the onion finely and cook in the butter till golden, adding the minced garlic half-way through. Skin the tomatoes and chop them. (Alternatively, use Italian tinned tomatoes, roughly crushed.) Add to the onion and cook slowly for 10 minutes. Season with salt and pepper and a little sugar. In summertime, a few leaves of chopped basil or tarragon can be added, or a pinch of dried marjoram at any time of the year. Serve as it is, or push through the coarse mesh of the vegetable mill for a smoother sauce.

CUSTARD SAUCE

2 egg yolks
2 Tbs home-made vanilla sugar, or
    plain castor sugar

½ pt milk
2-inch piece vanilla pod, if no
    vanilla sugar is available

Break the egg yolks into a bowl and beat with an electric beater or a wire whisk for 2 minutes, adding the vanilla sugar by degrees. When thick and creamy, heat the milk to boiling point and pour on, continuing to beat gently. Return to the pan and stir constantly over very gentle heat for a few minutes, until very slightly thickened. Remove from the heat immediately and keep warm over hot water. If to be served cold, stir often while cooling to prevent a skin forming. If you have no home-made vanilla sugar, heat the milk 20 minutes beforehand with a piece of vanilla pod in it. When just below boiling point, cover the pan and leave at the side of the fire for 20 minutes to allow the milk to infuse the flavour. Throw away the pod before mixing into the eggs. A most excellent sauce, this bears no relation to commercial custard, and is a delicious accompaniment to almost all English puddings, either hot or cold.

HOT JAM SAUCE

4 Tbs (or half a jar) strawberry jam
4 Tbs (or half a jar) raspberry jam
1 Tbs orange juice

1 Tbs lemon juice
½ Tbs brandy

Heat the jams very gently in a small pan, or over boiling water. Put them through the fine mesh of a food mill, or a baby-food strainer. Stir in the fruit juices and the brandy, re-heat, and serve. Good with castle puddings, pancakes, or freshly-made doughnuts. Children like it with vanilla ice-cream, but I find the mixture a bit too sweet.

RAISIN SAUCE

4 Tbs seedless raisins
¼ pt water
2 Tbs sugar

½ oz butter
1 Tbs brandy
½ gill cream

Put the raisins in a small pan with the water, sugar and butter. Simmer gently for about 10 minutes, till the raisins have swelled and become soft. Stir in the brandy and the cream and serve. Excellent with bread puddings and also with vanilla ice-cream.

RASPBERRY SAUCE

1 packet frozen raspberries
¼ lb castor sugar

1 Tbs brandy (optional)
1 Tbs thick cream

Make a syrup with the sugar and ¼ pt water. Add the defrosted raspberries and cook for 3 minutes. Pass through a sieve or the fine mesh of the vegetable mill. Stir in the brandy and the cream. Put in the freezer for 1 hour to chill well. Beat well and serve with strawberry ice-cream, strawberry fool, or mousse.

HOT TOFFEE SAUCE

4 Tbs golden syrup, or corn syrup
4 Tbs soft brown sugar

4 Tbs thick cream
1–2 Tbs lemon juice

Boil the syrup and the sugar together until they start to thicken. Add 2 Tbs cream and boil again. Stir in the remaining cream and lemon juice. Serve in a hot jug with vanilla ice-cream.

PUDDINGS AND SAVOURIES

BAKED APPLE DUMPLINGS
BOILED APPLE DUMPLINGS
BLAZING APPLES
CINNAMON APPLE CHARLOTTE
APPLE FRITTERS
CASTLE PUDDING I
CASTLE PUDDING II
PAIN PERDU
PLUM PUDDING I
PLUM PUDDING II
PRUNE MOUSSE
PRUNE JELLY
RASPBERRY MERINGUE
RICE PUDDING
SEVEN CUP PUDDING
WINE JELLY
CHEESE STRAWS
PARMESAN BACON

On Christmas Day of this year 1857 our villa saw a very unusual sight. My Father had given strictest charge that no difference whatever was to be made in our meals on that day; the dinner was to be neither more copious than usual nor less so. He was obeyed, but the servants, secretly rebellious, made a small plum pudding for themselves. (I discovered afterwards, with pain, that Miss Marks received a slice of it in her boudoir.) Early in the afternoon, the maids – of whom we were now advanced to keeping two – kindly remarked that 'the poor dear child ought to have a bit, anyhow', and wheedled me into the kitchen, where I ate a slice of plum pudding. Shortly I began to feel that pain inside which in my frail state was inevitable, and my conscience smote me violently. At length I could bear my spiritual anguish no longer, and bursting into the study I called out: 'Oh! Papa, Papa, I have eaten of flesh offered to idols!' It took some time, between my sobs, to explain what had happened. Then my Father sternly asked: 'Where is the accursed thing?' I explained that as much as was left of it was still on the kitchen table. He took me by the hand, and ran with me into the midst of the startled servants, seized what remained of the pudding, and with the plate in one hand and me still tight in the other, ran till we reached the dust-heap, when he flung the idolatrous confectionery into the middle of the ashes, and then raked it deep down into the mass. The suddenness, the violence, the velocity of this extraordinary act made an impression on my memory which nothing will ever efface.

FATHER AND SON, EDMUND GOSSE, HEINEMANN, 1907

BAKED APPLE DUMPLINGS

short pastry:

12 oz flour   6 oz butter
a pinch of salt   a little lemon juice
½ tsp sugar   1 egg yolk

2 Tbs raisins   2 Tbs soft brown sugar
1 Tbs brandy   1½ oz butter
6 eating apples, e.g. Granny Smith's   1 egg yolk
   or Coxes   castor sugar

Make the pastry, adding a drop of lemon juice and an egg yolk for richness.
Chill for 1 hour before using. Divide into 6 equal pieces and roll each one
out to a very thin circle. Peel the apples. Have the raisins soaked in brandy
and put 1 tsp in each cavity. Add 1 tsp soft brown sugar to each one and
top with a knob of butter. Lay an apple in the centre of each circle of
pastry and trim off four pieces to make a shape roughly like a Maltese cross.
Gather the four sides up, seal with beaten yolk of egg and bake for 20
minutes at 400°, then a further 20 minutes at 350°. Sprinkle with castor
sugar and serve with lightly whipped cream.

BOILED APPLE DUMPLINGS

pastry:

1 lb flour   a little milk
½ lb butter   1 egg yolk (optional)

6 dessert apples – Granny Smith's,   6 Tbs lemon or grapefruit
   for example   marmalade

Make the pastry, using the egg yolk for a richer mixture, and divide into 6
equal pieces. Roll each one out very thinly indeed and cut in the shape of a
cross. Peel the apples and remove the cores. Lay each apple on a piece of
pastry and fill the cavity with the marmalade. Wrap the ends of the pastry
over the apples, and seal with a little water. Have 6 squares of muslin and
sprinkle each one with flour. Lay a dumpling in each one, twist the muslin
loosely round it allowing room for the dumpling to swell, and tie the ends,

leaving them as long as possible to lift the dumplings out of the pan. Have a large pan of simmering water and drop the dumplings in. Keep boiling gently for 35–40 minutes, then lift out and unwrap. Lay one on each plate and serve with thick cream, unwhipped.

BLAZING APPLES

6 apples, small Bramleys or eating apples, e.g. Coxes or Granny Smith's

¼ lb sugar
apricot jam, about half a jar
4 Tbs rum

Choose a broad pan with a lid, large enough to fit in all the apples in one layer – a sauté pan is ideal. Put ¾ pint water in it with the sugar and bring to the boil. Simmer until the sugar has dissolved and a thin syrup is formed. Peel the apples and remove the cores. Fill the cavities with apricot jam and lay them in the syrup. There will not be enough to cover them but this does not matter; they will cook in the steam. Cover the pan and cook gently for 8–10 minutes, or until the apples are tender, watching them like a hawk as they can very quickly collapse if left a minute too long. In fact, it is a good thing to have a couple of extra apples in reserve in case one or two do flop. As soon as they are soft when pierced with a fine skewer, lift them out with a slotted spoon and lay them in a hot serving dish, again in one layer. Keep them hot while you reduce the juice by fast boiling till thick and syrupy. It does not matter if some of the jam has become mixed with it. Pour it over the apples. Just before serving, heat the rum in a ladle, light it, and pour over the apples. Serve while still flaming. Accompany with a jug of thick cream. A spectacular and delicious pudding; any remaining apples are also good eaten cold. If you have no rum, brandy or marc de Bourgogne can be used instead, or almost any liqueur for that matter.

CINNAMON APPLE CHARLOTTE

2 lb cooking apples
3 oz sugar
1 Tbs lemon juice
3 Tbs water

3 slices slightly stale bread
2 oz butter
2 oz castor sugar
1 tsp cinnamon

Slice the peeled and cored apples and stew them gently with the sugar, lemon juice and water in a covered pan till soft. Put them through the medium mesh of the food mill and keep hot in a shallow dish. Melt the butter without allowing it to burn. Cut the crusts off the bread and cut each slice in quarters. Brush each side of the pieces with the melted butter and dip them in the castor sugar and cinnamon, which you have mixed together on a plate. Lay them on a greased baking sheet and put in the oven for 15 minutes at 400°, turning them over half-way through. Watch to see they do not burn; they should be a golden brown. Lay them on top of the apple purée and serve with thick cream.

APPLE FRITTERS

batter:
3 oz flour
a pinch of salt

1 egg, separated
$\frac{1}{4}$ pint flat pale ale

3 hard green dessert apples, such as
   Granny Smith's

vanilla sugar, or castor sugar

Sift the flour with the salt into a large basin. Make a well in the middle and break in the egg yolk. Using a wire whisk, beat the egg yolk with the flour, pouring in the ale gradually at the same time. When all is smooth, leave to stand for 1–2 hours in a cool place. Just before using, beat the egg white until stiff and fold into the batter.

Peel the apples and remove the cores. Cut in slices about $\frac{1}{4}$ inch thick. Have a pan of deep oil heated to 360°. Dip the apple slices in the batter and drop them into the hot oil, only a few at a time, leaving room for them to float around without touching each other. After 2–3 minutes, turn them over with a slotted spoon, and leave another 2–3 minutes, so that they are golden brown on both sides. Lift out and drain on soft paper while you cook another batch. When drained, lay them on a flat platter and sprinkle with (home-made) vanilla sugar, or castor sugar.

CASTLE PUDDING I

3 oz butter
3 oz castor sugar (home-made
   vanilla sugar is excellent)

3 oz self-raising flour
2 medium eggs

Cream the butter and beat in the sugar by degrees. (If you have no vanilla sugar, use ordinary sugar and add 1 tsp grated lemon rind.) Stir in the flour and the beaten eggs alternately, a spoonful at a time. Mix lightly and pour into a buttered pudding basin which the mixture only fills by about three quarters. Cover with aluminium foil and place in a large saucepan with boiling water to come half-way up the basin. Cover the pan and cook for $1\frac{1}{2}$ hours, adding more boiling water to the pan when necessary. Turn out and serve with hot jam sauce (page 88), or golden syrup heated with a little lemon juice.

CASTLE PUDDING II

3 eggs
3 oz castor sugar
3 oz flour

1 tsp grated lemon rind, or use
   vanilla sugar
3 oz butter, semi-melted

Although the ingredients are almost the same as the preceding recipe, the method of cooking these puddings is quite different, and the result is also excellent.

Beat the eggs until very light and almost frothy, adding the sugar and lemon rind by degrees and beating continuously. Then shake in the flour, also by degrees, and lastly the semi-melted butter. When all is well mixed, pour it into small buttered moulds shaped like sand castles. Bake for 20 minutes at 350°. Turn out of their moulds to serve, and accompany with golden syrup heated with a little lemon juice, and a jug of cream.

PAIN PERDU

½ pt milk
2 Tbs home-made vanilla sugar, or
    plain sugar and a piece vanilla
    pod
6 large slices stale bread

2 eggs
butter
raisin sauce (page 88), or whipped
    cream

Heat the milk with the vanilla sugar. (If you do not have any, use ordinary sugar and add a 1-inch piece vanilla pod.) Bring to boiling point and reduce heat slightly. Cook gently until the sugar has melted, then leave to cool. (If using vanilla pod, throw away when the milk has completely cooled.) Cut the crusts off the bread and cut each slice in quarters. Lay the pieces in a shallow dish and pour over the milk. Turn them over and allow them to absorb the milk without becoming too soft. Beat the eggs and dip the slices in the mixture. Fry on both sides in butter until golden. Serve sprinkled with castor sugar. Accompany with raisin sauce (page 88), or a bowl of lightly whipped cream.

PLUM PUDDING I

¼ lb soft white breadcrumbs
½ lb suet
½ lb currants
½ lb raisins
¼ lb sugar
2 oz candied peel

grated rind of ½ lemon
½ tsp ground nutmeg
½ tsp mixed spice
a pinch of salt
4 eggs
a liqueur glass of brandy

Mix all the ingredients except for the eggs and the brandy in a large deep bowl. When very thoroughly mixed, beat the eggs and stir them in. Mix in the brandy and put in a buttered pudding basin. Cover with aluminium foil or a cloth and boil or steam for 4–6 hours. This makes one large pudding which I usually eat straight away, for a winter's weekend lunch party, with a home-made custard sauce. It will serve 8–10 people. It makes a delicious light, moist pudding, less firm than the usual plum pudding. It can equally well be stored and re-steamed on Christmas Day.

PLUM PUDDING II

This is the pudding I always make at Christmas time; it is unusual in that it contains neither flour nor sugar, and it makes an extremely good pudding. Those who like a very rich, moist pudding may not fancy it, but I find it quite rich enough.

$1\frac{1}{2}$ lb seedless raisins
$\frac{1}{2}$ lb mixed candied peel
$\frac{1}{2}$ lb glacé cherries
$\frac{1}{4}$ lb blanched almonds
$\frac{3}{4}$ lb shredded suet

$\frac{3}{4}$ lb soft white breadcrumbs
8 eggs
$\frac{1}{4}$ pt Guinness
6 Tbs brandy

Halve the raisins if they are large, chop the peel, halve the cherries, and chop the almonds. Mix all together with the suet and the breadcrumbs. Stir in the well-beaten eggs, the stout and the brandy. The mixture can be left at this stage for a few hours, or even until the next day as this allows the flavours to develop, and the mixing and the cooking together make a long day's work. When ready to cook, pack the pudding mixture into three $1\frac{1}{2}$ pint pudding basins which have been well buttered. (Charms should be added at this stage if used; they are hard to find nowadays but they can still be bought at Harrods in the cake department. If one pudding has charms, remember to distinguish it in some way, as weeks later it may be impossible to remember which it was.) The bowls should not be filled too full; there should be a good inch left empty at the top. Cover with a buttered piece of aluminium foil and wrap in a clean piece of white linen – part of an old sheet will do. Have a very large pan ready with enough boiling water to come half-way up the bowls. Lay each bowl carefully on an upturned saucer – use old chipped ones as the long boiling destroys the surface of the china – and cover the pan. Bring quickly back to the boil and keep boiling steadily for 6 hours, adding more boiling water as needed to keep the level up roughly once an hour. When the time is up, lift out the puddings and leave to cool; if they are not all needed, one can be eaten straight away. The others should be stored in a cool place like a wine cellar as soon as they are cold. On Christmas Day the pudding should be boiled again in the same way, for 4–6 hours. To serve, turn out onto a heated dish, stick a small sprig of holly in the top, and pour some flaming brandy over it just before bringing it to the table. (Heat 3 Tbs brandy gently in a ladle over the gas flame, then set light to it.) Each of these puddings will serve 6–8 people, but if a larger pudding is needed the mixture can be divided between two larger bowls, or one very large one and one smaller one.

PRUNE MOUSSE

½ lb prunes
cold tea
2 oz sugar

2 Tbs brandy or 1 Tbs lemon juice
¼ pt thick cream
3 egg whites

Cook the prunes until very soft in the cold tea and the sugar. Lift out of the juice and remove the stones. Chop the flesh and put in the blender with some of the juice, enough to make a fairly thick purée which is free of lumps. Add the brandy or the lemon juice to taste. Whip the cream and fold in. Then beat the egg whites until stiff and fold in also. Chill in the refrigerator.

PRUNE JELLY

2 8-fl oz bottles S & W prune juice
   (an excellent American brand
   found in many London stores)
1 Tbs castor sugar

2 Tbs lemon juice
2 Tbs orange juice
1 packet (½ oz) gelatine
½ pt thick cream

Add the sugar to the prune juice, then the fruit juices. Melt the gelatine in ½ gill hot water and mix with the juices. Pour through a strainer into a ring mould of 1-pint capacity and chill in the refrigerator. As it is already cold it will only take a couple of hours to set. Turn out onto a flat plate and fill the centre with lightly whipped cream.

RASPBERRY MERINGUE

3 egg whites
6 oz castor sugar

2 packets frozen raspberries without
   sugar
½ pt double cream

Beat the egg whites until stiff, then fold in the sifted castor sugar gradually, continuing to beat. When thick and creamy, spoon onto a round of oiled aluminium foil on a baking sheet. Smooth out slightly into a thick circle with a palette knife. Put in the middle of the oven heated to 175° and leave for 2 hours, watching occasionally to make sure all is well. If it colours unevenly, it should be turned round from time to time. It should turn a delicate straw colour, nothing darker. Remove from the oven and cool. Remove from the foil – sometimes this seems impossible without breaking the meringue, but don't despair. If it's still whole or roughly so, lay it on a flat dish and cover with the lightly whipped cream which will camouflage a few cracks. Take the raspberries out of the freezer 1 hour beforehand so they are only just defrosted and lay them one by one on top of the cream. If the meringue breaks into several pieces, break it up even more, and make layers of meringue pieces, whipped cream, and raspberries in a soufflé dish. This is just as good and only slightly less pretty.

RICE PUDDING

2 oz Carolina rice
1 oz castor sugar (home-made
   vanilla sugar if possible)

1 oz butter
1 pt milk
grated nutmeg (optional)

Wash the rice and drain it. Butter a china pie dish and put the rice in it. Add the sugar and the butter cut in small pieces. Pour on the milk and give a stir with a fork. If liked, sprinkle grated nutmeg over the top. Cook in a very low oven – 225° works well with my oven – for 2 hours. You may have to adjust the timing and the heat to suit your oven as thermostats are not always accurate. When ready, the top should be golden brown and the milk not quite all absorbed, although this is a matter of choice. Excellent either hot or cold, with cream, stewed fruit, or on its own. A welcome relief after too much rich food. Serves 4–5.

SEVEN CUP PUDDING

This is an old-fashioned pudding recipe which my Scottish grandmother gave to my mother when she married. The measurements are based on volume rather than weight; choose a teacup holding about 6 fluid ounces as your measure.

1 teacup soft white breadcrumbs	2 tsp ground ginger
1 teacup shredded suet	1 tsp ground cinnamon
1 teacup sultanas	1 tsp mixed spice
1 teacup currants	a pinch of salt
1 teacup sugar	1 tsp bicarbonate of soda
1 teacup flour	1 egg
2 oz chopped mixed peel	approx. $\frac{1}{4}$ pt milk
2 oz coarsely chopped or grated almonds	1 tsp wine vinegar

Mix all the ingredients together except for the egg, milk, baking soda and vinegar. Break the egg into a measuring jug and make up to 6 fl oz with milk. Stir into the mixture. Dissolve the baking soda in the vinegar for a few moments, then stir into the pudding mixture. Mix all together well, then pour into a buttered pudding basin and steam (covered, set in a large pan of boiling water half-way up the sides of the bowl) for 4–6 hours. Turn out and serve with custard sauce (see page 87). Serves 6–8.

An excellent spicy pudding, less rich and heavy than a plum pudding, but can be used as a substitute for one if required, with brandy butter instead of custard sauce.

WINE JELLY

4 oz sugar	1 lemon
$\frac{1}{2}$ lb redcurrant jelly	$\frac{1}{2}$ bottle red wine
1 orange	1 packet ($\frac{1}{2}$ oz) gelatine

Put the sugar in a small pan with $\frac{1}{4}$ pt water. Add the redcurrant jelly, the grated rind, and the juice of the orange and the lemon. Heat gently, and stir until the sugar has melted. Pour through a strainer to get rid of any lumps, and return to the clean pan. Pour in the red wine and stir over gentle heat till all is mixed. Melt the gelatine in $\frac{1}{2}$ gill hot water and add to the mixture. Stir over low heat till blended smoothly, and strain once more. Pour into a ring mould and leave to set. Put in the refrigerator overnight, and turn out onto a flat platter to serve. Fill the centre with lightly whipped cream.

CHEESE STRAWS

4 oz flour
2 oz butter
1½ oz grated Gruyère } or 3 oz grated Parmesan
1½ oz grated Parmesan }
2 egg yolks
1 tsp mustard powder
salt
cayenne pepper
a little extra grated Parmesan

Sieve the flour and rub in the butter, cut in small pieces. Add the grated cheese and mix with the blade of a knife. Add the mustard powder, a pinch of salt and cayenne. Stir in the beaten egg yolks and enough iced water to make a firm paste. Leave in a cool place for 1 hour, then roll out to about ⅛ inch thick. Cut either into sticks, about 2 inches long by ¼ inch wide, or small rounds. Bake on a greased baking sheet for about 5 minutes at 400°. Sprinkle with grated Parmesan immediately on taking out of the oven. Serve hot, with a clear soup, or as a savoury. If serving as a savoury, arrange a little bundle of the sticks stuck through a ring of the same mixture for each person. (Cut out a circle about 2½ inches round, then a smaller circle within the same piece about 2 inches round, leaving a ring of pastry.)

PARMESAN BACON

6 oz green streaky bacon, cut at no 3 (very thin indeed)
½ gill thick cream
2 oz very fine white breadcrumbs (freshly made, but not too soft)
2 oz grated Parmesan

Brush each rasher with cream on both sides. Mix the breadcrumbs and the cheese, and dip each rasher in the mixture, coating them evenly on both sides. Grill them gently so they become crisp and golden brown without allowing them to burn. Drain briefly on absorbent paper and serve immediately on a flat dish. A light and appetising savoury, a good alternative to a sweet dish after a rich meal.

BREAD, BISCUITS AND CAKES

CHRISTMAS BREAD
CHOCOLATE CAKE
ICEBOX COOKIES
CHOCOLATE ICEBOX COOKIES
PINWHEEL COOKIES
LADY MORAY'S PLUM CAKE
CHRISTMAS DOUGHNUTS
CHRISTMAS SNOWBALLS

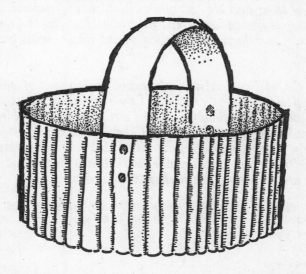

A fat brown goose lay at one end of the table, and at the other end, on a bed of creased paper strewn with sprigs of parsley, lay a great ham, stripped of its outer skin and peppered over with crust crumbs, a neat paper frill round its shin, and beside this was a round of spiced beef. Between these rival ends ran parallel lines of side-dishes: two little minsters of jelly, red and yellow; a shallow dish full of blocks of blancmange and red jam, a large green leaf-shaped dish with a stalk-shaped handle on which lay bunches of purple raisins and peeled almonds, a companion dish on which lay a solid rectangle of Smyrna figs, a dish of custard topped with grated nutmeg, a small bowl full of chocolates and sweets wrapped in gold and silver papers and a glass vase in which stood some tall celery stalks. In the centre of the table there stood, as sentries to a fruit stand which upheld a pyramid of oranges and American apples, two squat old-fashioned decanters of cut glass, one containing port and the other dark sherry. On the closed square piano a pudding in a huge yellow dish lay waiting, and behind it were three squads of bottles of stout and ale and minerals, drawn up according to the colours of their uniforms, the first two black, with brown and red labels, the third and smallest squad white, with transverse sashes.

While Gabriel and Miss Daly exchanged plates of goose and plates of ham and spiced beef, Lily went from guest to guest with a dish of hot floury potatoes wrapped in a napkin white. This was Mary Jane's idea and she had also suggested apple sauce for the goose, but Aunt Kate had said that plain roast goose without any apple sauce had always been good enough for her and she hoped she might never eat worse.

THE DEAD, FROM *THE DUBLINERS,* JAMES JOYCE,
JONATHAN CAPE, 1914

CHRISTMAS BREAD

1¾ lb flour
1 tsp salt
1 oz fresh yeast, or ½ oz dried yeast
3 oz lard
2 eggs
approx. 6 fl oz milk
½ lb raisins

¼ lb currants
¼ lb sultanas
2 oz cut mixed peel
6 oz sugar
1 Tbs black treacle
1 tsp mixed ground nutmeg, cloves
    and cinnamon

Put the flour in a large bowl with the salt and leave in a warm place. Put the yeast in a cup with 2 Tbs tepid water and leave in the same warm place for 10 minutes. Cut the lard in small pieces and rub into the flour. Beat the eggs and add enough tepid milk and water to make up to ¾ pint. Make a well in the middle of the flour and tip in first the yeast, then the eggs, milk and water. Mix roughly and put back in the warm place to rise for 30 minutes. Meanwhile, measure all the dried fruit and put in another bowl in the warmth. When the ½ hour is up, turn out the flour mixture and knead well, then mix in the dried fruit, the sugar and the treacle. Mix thoroughly, then leave to rise again for 2 hours. Divide the mixture between two large loaf tins, well buttered and sprinkled with flour, or lined with buttered greaseproof paper to be on the safe side. Return to the warmth for 20 minutes, then put in a moderate oven (340°) for 1¼ hours.

This delicious spiced fruit bread will keep well wrapped in a cloth and stored in a tin. It is excellent with butter for tea. I make it instead of a Christmas cake, which seems to me too like Christmas pudding.

CHOCOLATE CAKE

3½ oz butter
4 oz plain cooking chocolate
4 eggs
a pinch of salt

1 lb castor sugar, half vanilla sugar
    if possible
4 oz flour

Cut the chocolate into small pieces and melt with the butter in a bowl over a pan of boiling water. As soon as it has melted, mix together and remove from the pan to cool. 1 hour later, beat the eggs very well and gradually beat in the sugar and the pinch of salt. Stir in the melted chocolate, then fold in the sifted flour. Mix quickly and lightly rather than thoroughly, then pour into a buttered tin. I use a square tin measuring 10 inches by $1\frac{1}{2}$ inches deep, which is ideal. Bake for about 35 minutes, but this depends somewhat on the shape of the tin you use. Cool in the tin, then cut in squares. I cut mine in 9 large pieces, or in 12 slightly smaller ones. Serve with a bowl of whipped cream as a pudding, or as a cake for tea. If the individual pieces are wrapped in foil as soon as cooled, they are ideal for picnics. Alternatively, the whole tin can be covered in foil and tightly sealed, to keep it fresh for two or three days. It should be slightly chewy in the middle, not dry all through.

ICEBOX COOKIES

$\frac{1}{2}$ lb castor sugar $\frac{1}{4}$ tsp salt
4 oz butter $1\frac{1}{2}$ tsp baking powder
6 oz plain flour

Sieve the sugar. Cream the butter and beat in the sugar. (If possible, use a proportion of vanilla sugar.) Sieve the flour with the salt and the baking powder. Stir into the butter and sugar cream. When well mixed, divide the mixture into two pieces and form them into rolls about $1\frac{1}{2}$–2 inches in diameter. Wrap them in foil and place in the refrigerator. Leave for at least 12 hours before using. They will keep for several weeks. When ready to use, have the oven heated at 400° and lightly grease a baking sheet. Take the rolls out of the refrigerator and cut in very thin slices. Lay them on the baking sheet without allowing them to come too close to each other as they spread slightly in the cooking. Bake for 4–5 minutes, till golden brown. This mixture can also be frozen very successfully. Excellent to serve with ice-cream, fruit fools, or just with tea or coffee.

CHOCOLATE ICEBOX COOKIES

Make as for icebox cookies, adding 2 oz plain chocolate. Break the chocolate into small pieces and set in a small bowl over simmering water till melted, then set aside to cool. Add to the rest of the mixture after adding the flour. Cook in the same way.

PINWHEEL COOKIES

Make the biscuit mixture as for icebox cookies and divide it into 2 halves. Take 1 oz plain chocolate and melt it over hot water, then allow it to cool. Stir it into ½ of the mixture and chill slightly until firm enough to handle. Then roll out the 2 parts in similar sized and shaped rectangles, about ⅛ inch thick. Lay the chocolate rectangle on top of the plain one and roll them up like a Swiss roll. Wrap in foil and chill for at least 12 hours. The next day, slice and cook as for icebox cookies.

LADY MORAY'S PLUM CAKE

½ lb butter	1½ tsp ground nutmeg
½ lb soft brown sugar	¼ lb ground almonds
2 Tbs treacle	½ lb currants
4 medium eggs	½ lb raisins
¾ lb flour	½ lb sultanas
1 tsp baking powder	½ gill milk
1½ tsp ground cloves	juice of 1 orange
1½ tsp ground cinnamon	

Cream the butter and beat in the sugar gradually. Stir in the treacle, mixing well. Sift the flour. Break one egg at a time into a cup, beat with a fork, then mix into the creamed butter and sugar. Fold in a spoonful of flour after each egg to prevent curdling. When all the eggs are incorporated, add the baking powder and the spices to the remaining flour and fold into the mixture. Stir in the ground almonds, then the currants, raisins and sultanas. Last of all, stir in the milk and the orange juice. Have 2 tins measuring roughly 8 inches by 4, and butter them well. Divide the mixture between them and put in the middle of the oven, pre-heated to 325°. Bake for 2½ hours. After 1 hour, cover the tins loosely with a piece of aluminium foil to prevent the cakes from getting too brown.

This was my grandmother's recipe; a rich spiced fruit cake of this sort was often handed round with the cheese at luncheon parties in Scotland. It takes an hour to make and is quite tiring, but it can be made well in advance and is a useful stand-by over the holiday.

CHRISTMAS DOUGHNUTS

These little cakes are made in Holland at Christmas time, and eaten hot with mulled wine.

400 gr (14 oz) flour	200 gr (7 oz) mixed currants,
a pinch of salt	raisins, angelica
30 gr (1 oz) yeast	the rind of ½ orange
2 eggs	3 sour apples
4½ dl (¾ pint) lukewarm milk	

Sieve the flour with the salt into a warm bowl. Put the yeast with a little of the milk in a cup in a warm place and leave for 10 minutes to prove. Chop the angelica, peel and core the apples and chop very finely indeed. Pare the orange rind thinly and chop also. Pour the yeast into a well in the middle of the flour. Beat the eggs with the remaining milk and pour into the flour as well. Mix thoroughly, knead a few times and mix in the dried fruit, minced apples, and orange rind. Put back in the bowl, cover with a damp cloth, and leave in a warm place for about 1 hour till well risen. Have a pan of deep oil heated to about 360°. Using two large spoons, drop round balls of the dough into the oil, using one as a test. The oil must be the right temperature if they are to be cooked through at the same time as they are browning on the outside. Drain on a cloth or soft paper, sprinkle with castor sugar and serve. They are also good cold.

CHRISTMAS SNOWBALLS

My sister found this recipe in an old cookery book just as I was completing this book, so I am including it as it sounds amusing, although I have not had time to try it myself.

Any white cake mixture can be used. Have ready some small round-bottomed cake tins, greased and dusted with a mixture of flour and sugar. Half fill them with the mixture and bake at 375° for about 15 minutes, till lightly browned and firm to the touch. Turn out to cool. If necessary, cut a slice off the tops to make them level, then put two together with a layer of jelly between, to form a ball. Or, hollow out the middles slightly and fill with whipped cream before putting together. Cover with plain white icing, holding them on a fork or skewer. Then roll in desiccated coconut mixed with castor sugar. Allow to dry and garnish with sprigs of holly.

PRESERVES, ETC.

BRANDY BUTTER
CUMBERLAND SAUCE
MINCEMEAT
PEACHES IN BRANDY
PRUNES IN WINE
SALTED ALMONDS
SUGAR SYRUP
VANILLA SUGAR

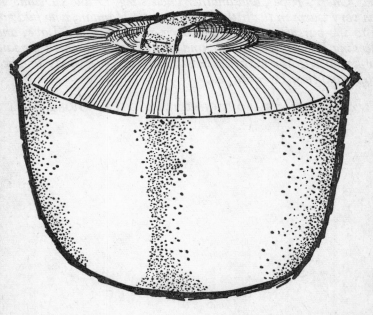

And then, at Christmas tea, the recovered uncles would be jolly over their mince-pies; and the great iced cake loomed in the centre of the table like a marble grave. Auntie Hannah laced her tea with rum, because it was only once a year. And in the evening, there was music. An uncle played the fiddle, a cousin sang 'Cherry Ripe', and another uncle sang 'Drake's Drum.' It was very warm in the little house. Auntie Hannah, who had got on to the parsnip wine, sang a song about Rejected Love, and Bleeding Hearts, and Death, and then another in which she said her heart was like a Bird's Nest; and then everybody laughed again, and then I went to bed.

CONVERSATIONS ABOUT CHRISTMAS, DYLAN THOMAS, 1954

BRANDY BUTTER

¼ lb unsalted butter   3–4 Tbs brandy
¼ lb castor sugar

Cream the butter until very pale and smooth. Add the sugar gradually,
beating all the time. When amalgamated, add the brandy very slowly, a
few drops at a time, while beating continuously. After 3 Tbs have been
added, taste for flavouring. Be careful adding the last spoon, as it curdles
and separates very easily. Pile into a small bowl and chill in the refrigerator.
It keeps well. This sauce can also be made with rum, or with bourbon,
which is excellent. The traditional accompaniment to plum pudding, it is
good served with all rich fruit puddings and with mince pies. A simpler
alternative is to beat 1–2 Tbs brandy into a bowl of lightly whipped cream.
A little castor sugar can be added at the same time.

CUMBERLAND SAUCE

1 shallot   1 tsp French mustard
2 oranges   1 glass (¼ pt) port
1 lemon   1 tsp arrowroot
½ lb redcurrant jelly

Chop the shallot very finely indeed. Pare the rind of 1 orange and the
lemon. Cut it in very thin strips and put in a small pan with the minced
shallot. Cover with cold water, bring to the boil, and simmer for 5 minutes.
Drain. Put the jelly in a small bowl over a pan of boiling water. Stir until
melted and smooth; it may be necessary to put it through a small strainer
(a baby food strainer is ideal) to make it absolutely smooth. Stir in the
mustard, the port, the juice of the oranges and the lemon, and the blanched
rind and shallot. Simmer for 4–5 minutes, then stir in the arrowroot mixed
to a paste with 2 tsp water. Simmer for 1 more minute, then pour into a jar
and leave to cool. Close the jar tightly when cold and do not use for two or
three days, if possible. It will keep for a couple of months, and makes a
good present, especially when accompanied by a small pâté. Serve cold,
with cold meat, ham, game, or pâté.

MINCEMEAT

2 large lemons
6 oz rump steak (optional)
12 oz hard green dessert apples
12 oz raisins
12 oz currants
12 oz candied peel
12 oz sugar
12 oz shredded suet

½ tsp ground nutmeg
½ tsp ground cinnamon
½ tsp allspice
½ tsp ground cloves
¼ tsp salt
a few turns of the pepper mill
2 liqueur glasses brandy (about 6 fl oz)

Grate the rind and squeeze the juice of the lemons. Grill the steak quickly, or sear in a very hot pan. Cool, then chop it finely, being careful to save the juice. Peel and core the apples and chop them finely. Mix all the dry ingredients in a large bowl, moisten with the lemon juice and the brandy. Leave the bowl covered in a cool place for a few hours, then pack the mixture into jars, close tightly, and leave for several days before using. This amount will fill three 2 lb Kilner jars. They will keep for several weeks in a cool place.

Old English recipes for mincemeat always included meat, either beef or tongue, or a mixture of both, and most American recipes still do. Like many other medieval English habits, it seems to have been preserved faithfully in the United States, while in England it has been allowed to lapse. The idea may not appeal to those who are not already familiar with it, but I promise it improves the flavour without making it meaty. It can be omitted, however. This is a really excellent recipe, useful for giving as presents as well as for home consumption.

PEACHES IN BRANDY

4 peaches, white-fleshed if possible
½ lb lump or granulated sugar
4 Tbs brandy

1 piece cinnamon stick
4 cloves

Make a syrup by boiling ½ pt water with the sugar, cinnamon and cloves. When the sugar has melted, put in the peaches, cut in half and with the stones removed. After 3 minutes, lift them out and skin them. (If totally ripe, they may be skinned before poaching.) Return them to the syrup and poach for another 4 minutes. Leave to cool in the syrup. The next day, lift out the peaches and put them into glass jars. Boil up the syrup till slightly reduced, mix with the brandy and pour over the peaches, removing the cinnamon and cloves. Leave to cool, then close the jars tightly. Do not eat for a week or two. These make a nice present, or a delicious treat to serve to friends. Accompany them with a crème brûlée, a cold creamy rice pudding, or a crème caramel.

PRUNES IN WINE

Take the best quality prunes, remove the stones carefully, and pack into a small glass jar with a well-fitting lid. Fill up the jar with a good red wine. Close the jar securely and leave for 10 days. Serve from the jar, with a thin fork to get them out, with the coffee at the end of a meal.

SALTED ALMONDS

whole almonds, blanched and peeled	butter salt

If the almonds are not already blanched, this is easily done. Put them in a bowl and pour over boiling water to cover. After a minute or two, take them out, a few at a time, and rub off the skins between the fingers. Dry them thoroughly in a cloth and they are ready for salting.

Heat some butter in a frying pan and when it is very hot, put in the almonds. Fry them quickly, turning frequently, until they are a pale golden – more of a straw colour than a brown – on both sides. Drain very well indeed on soft paper, then lay them on a plate and sprinkle with salt. Some people add cayenne pepper as well, but I prefer them without. If possible, they should be eaten the same day as made. They can be kept for a few days, however, if stored in air-tight containers, or carefully sealed in little packets of aluminium foil.

SUGAR SYRUP

¼ lb sugar   ¼ pt water

Put the sugar and the water in a small pan and bring to the boil. Simmer for 2–3 minutes, until the sugar has completely melted, then pour into a small jug and leave to cool. When cold, store in the refrigerator. Use for sweetening cocktails. (Dry sugar does not melt satisfactorily in cold drinks, and thus fails to sweeten the cocktail.)

VANILLA SUGAR

Put 3 vanilla pods in a tall glass jar with a tightly fitting stopper. Fill up with castor sugar, and leave for at least 10 days before using. Replenish the sugar as you use it. The pods will keep their flavour for about a year, when they should be renewed. This is a most useful flavouring for sweet sauces; I never trust the vanilla sugar one sometimes sees in small packets in the shops. If I run out of my own, I use a piece of vanilla pod to flavour the liquid part of the dish instead, when possible.

CHRISTMAS DRINKS

OLD-FASHIONED
WHISKEY MAC   WHISKEY SOUR

TO FROST A COCKTAIL GLASS
COCKTAIL No I
COCKTAIL No II   COCKTAIL No III

BELLINI   BLACK VELVET
BLOODY MARY   BUCK'S FIZZ
BULLSHOT   CHAMPAGNE COCKTAIL
DAIQUIRI   PINK GIN FIZZ
WHITE LADY   MULLED WINE
PEPPER VODKA   RASPBERRY (OR
STRAWBERRY) VODKA   SLOE GIN

CIDER CUP   CLARET CUP
GINGER ALE CUP   WHITE WINE CUP

EGGNOG
IRISH COFFEE

The uncles sat in front of the fire, took off their collars, loosened all buttons, put their large moist hands over their watch-chains, groaned a little, and slept. Mothers and aunts and sisters scuttled to and fro, bearing tureens. The dog was sick. Auntie Beattie had to have three aspirins, but Auntie Hannah, who liked port, stood in the middle of the snow-bound back yard, singing like a big-bosomed thrush.

CONVERSATIONS ABOUT CHRISTMAS, DYLAN THOMAS, 1954

OLD-FASHIONED

A truly delicious drink, a cocktail made with American bourbon as opposed to Scotch whiskey. It is festive and warming, and extremely strong. For each cocktail:

1 tsp sugar syrup
1–2 dashes angostura bitters
3–4 lumps ice
bourbon

$\frac{1}{2}$ thin slice orange
$\frac{1}{2}$ thin slice lemon
1 maraschino cherry on a cocktail
   stick

Take a highball glass – a short squat tumbler – and put the sugar syrup in the bottom. Add the angostura bitters and mix. Put in 3 or 4 lumps ice and fill $\frac{3}{4}$ full with bourbon. Mix with a long spoon, add the fruit, and serve.

WHISKEY MAC

1 part ginger wine   2 parts Scotch whiskey

I like to mix these over ice, although this is not technically correct. A good warming winter drink.

WHISKEY SOUR

1 part lemon juice   4 parts bourbon
$\frac{1}{2}$ part sugar syrup

Mix over ice and serve in a cocktail glass.

TO FROST A COCKTAIL GLASS

Rub the rim of the glass with a cut section of lemon, so that it is well moistened with the juice, then dip it in castor sugar. Leave to dry.

COCKTAIL No. I

2 parts Dubonnet
2 parts unsweetened grapefruit
   juice

1 part vodka
a dash of Cointreau
a sprig of mint (when available)

Mix in a jug with plenty of ice and, in summertime, some sprigs of fresh mint. This cocktail is beautifully cloudy and has a strange flavour that is hard to identify.

COCKTAIL No. II

1 part Campari

1 part orange juice

Mix well with plenty of ice.

COCKTAIL No. III

1 part Cinzano (sweet)
1 part Campari

1 part lemon juice
a dash of vodka

Mix well with lots of ice in a jug. A sharp, refreshing cocktail for those who like Campari; a beautiful cherry red colour.

BELLINI

1 part champagne   1 part peach juice

Like the Buck's fizz, this cocktail which originated in Harry's Bar in Venice is sometimes made with 2 parts champagne to 1 of fruit juice. The peach juice must be freshly made; this is easy when you use a juice extractor.

BLACK VELVET

1 part very dry champagne   1 part stout

Have both the champagne and the stout well iced, and mix carefully, remembering that the mixture will froth up.

BLOODY MARY

2 parts V8 vegetable juice   a dash angostura bitters
2 parts vodka   the slightest dash Tabasco or chilli
1 part lemon juice   sauce

Mix well with lots of ice. Tomato juice can be used instead of V8, and generally is, but the mixed vegetable juice gives a better flavour.

BUCK'S FIZZ

1 part champagne   1 part orange juice

Some people make this with 2 parts champagne to 1 of orange juice.

BULLSHOT

1 part Campbell's tinned beef
   bouillon, or Crosse & Blackwell's
   consommé
1 part vodka

½ part lemon juice
a dash of Worcester sauce
a dash of angostura bitters

Mix well with lots of ice.

CHAMPAGNE COCKTAIL

For each cocktail:
1 lump sugar

2 dashes angostura bitters
champagne

Put a lump of sugar in a chilled saucer-shaped champagne glass. Put 2 dashes angostura bitters onto the sugar and fill up with iced champagne. Do not use champagne of the best quality; a second class champagne wil be just as good.

DAIQUIRI

1 part fresh lime (or lemon) juice
½ part sugar syrup

4 parts Bacardi white rum
1 maraschino cherry (optional)

Mix the sugar syrup with the fruit juice in a jug. Add plenty of crushed ice. Pour on the rum, mix very well and serve in chilled cocktail glasses, with a maraschino cherry if you like. The glasses may be frosted (see page 120). Lime juice is particularly delicious, but when limes are unobtainable, lemons make a perfectly good substitute.

PINK GIN FIZZ

1 part sugar syrup
a dash of angostura bitters
2 parts lemon juice

3 parts gin
soda water

Put the sugar syrup in a tall glass and add the angostura. Mix well, then add the lemon juice and gin. Add plenty of ice and fill up with soda water, or a fizzy mineral such as Perrier.

WHITE LADY

1 part lemon juice
1 part Cointreau

2 parts gin

Mix well over ice and serve, with a maraschino cherry as garnish. The rim of the glass may be frosted (see page 120).

MULLED WINE

the peel of 1 lemon
the peel of 1 orange
6 cloves
1 stick cinnamon
½ nutmeg

12 lumps sugar
1½ bottles claret, or claret-type
  wine
1 liqueur glass brandy (optional)

Put the lemon and orange peel, the cloves, cinnamon, nutmeg and sugar in a saucepan with ½ pint water. Bring to the boil and cook till the sugar is melted. Add the wine and bring back to boiling point. Add brandy if liked. Strain into a hot jug or bowl.

PEPPER VODKA

about 6 chilli peppers   1 bottle vodka

Have some small bottles of clear glass and put 2 or 3 peppers in each one.
Fill up with pure vodka and close tightly. Leave for at least 10 days, then
drink, or give as presents. Leave the peppers in the bottles. Chill before
drinking; the cold makes a pleasant contrast with the heat of the peppers.
For a special effect, the bottle can be frozen in a block of ice, by placing in
a jar slightly larger than itself filled with water, then leaving – but not too
long – in the freezer. The water will freeze before the vodka.

RASPBERRY (OR STRAWBERRY) VODKA

6 oz raspberries, strawberries, or   1 bottle vodka
fraises du bois

Have the fruit well picked-over, clean and dry. Put it in a wide-mouthed
bottle or jar and fill up with vodka. If using small bottles, allow 2 oz fruit
to 8–10 fl oz vodka. Use the best and purest vodka you can afford. Seal or
cork the bottles tightly and leave for at least 10 days. Strain into clean
bottles, throwing away the fruit which looks less pretty now than it did at
first, and seal again. Useful as presents, this is a home-made version of the
delicious French and Swiss eaux-de-vie de framboises. The finished drink
is a pretty pale pink, and should be bottled in clear glass bottles; a $\frac{1}{2}$ pint
bottle makes a useful small present.

SLOE GIN

6 bottles dry gin   2$\frac{1}{2}$ lb lump sugar
3 quarts sloes

Have one huge earthenware crock or jar – capacity 2 gallons – or two smaller ones. Stick the head of a strong darning or embroidery needle into a cork, and prick each washed sloe two or three times. Drop them into the crock which you have half filled with gin, add the sugar, and close the jar. Leave for 2½–3 months – it will be just ready in time to bottle for Christmas – shaking the crock twice a week, or turning it on its side and rolling it over. It is then ready to put into bottles.

Sloes are ripe at the beginning of October. They are like a small bitter plum or damson, and can be found growing in profusion in wooded areas of southern England. This recipe makes a really excellent drink, far better then the commercially made one, ideal for Christmas drinking or to give as presents. It is fun finding pretty bottles in which to bottle your gin and designing the labels. Sloe gin is extremely strong and should be drunk in small glasses before meals, as an aperitif. It can also be made in half quantities.

CIDER CUP

2½ fl oz sugar syrup
2½ fl oz lemon juice
¼ pt orange juice
2 fl oz applejack or calvados (for a slightly stronger cup)
1 large bottle (32 fl oz) dry cider

½ orange, sliced
½ lemon, sliced
4 strips cucumber peel, or borage in season
a few maraschino cherries, or strawberries in season

Mix the sugar syrup, fruit juices, and calvados (if used) in a large jug and chill for two hours in the refrigerator. Have the cider also chilling. When ready to serve, put about 8 ice cubes in the jug and pour over the cider. Stir and serve. Can be made just as easily in double or triple quantities.

CLARET CUP

6 fl oz sugar syrup
6 fl oz lemon juice
¾ pt orange juice
3 fl oz orange curaçao
3 fl oz brandy

2 bottles claret, or claret-type red wine
6 long strips cucumber peel
1 large bottle (32 fl oz) fizzy mineral water, e.g. Perrier or Vichy

Find a largish jug that will fit in your refrigerator and, some hours before serving, mix the sugar syrup with the fruit juices. Add the spirits and wine, and put in the cucumber peel. Leave for an hour, then put in the refrigerator for another 2 hours. Just before serving, add ice and the fizzy water. (Soda water can be used, but aerated mineral water is much better.) Makes enough for 10–12 people.

GINGER ALE CUP

2½ fl oz sugar syrup
2½ fl oz lemon juice
¼ pt orange juice
2½ fl oz ginger wine

½ orange, sliced
½ lemon, sliced
4 strips cucumber peel
2 large (17 oz) bottles ginger ale

Mix the sugar syrup, the fruit juices and the ginger wine in a large jug and chill in the refrigerator. Have the ginger ale also chilling. Add the cucumber peel. At the last moment, put lots of ice cubes in the jug, pour over the ginger ale and garnish with the sliced fruit. A delicious cup with practically no alcoholic content. Can easily be made in double quantities, or even more.

WHITE WINE CUP

6 fl oz sugar syrup
6 fl oz lemon juice
¾ pt orange juice
3 fl oz orange curaçao
3 fl oz brandy

2 bottles sauternes, moselle, or
   other Rhein wine
6 long strips cucumber peel
1 large bottle Vichy, Perrier, or
   other fizzy mineral water.

Mix the sugar syrup, the fruit juices, the spirits and wine in a jug. Add the cucumber peel and put in the refrigerator for 2–3 hours. When ready to serve, add plenty of ice and the mineral water. (Soda water can be substituted if necessary.) Makes enough for 10–12 people. Also excellent in summer time, this cup has a delicious fresh, fruity taste, not unlike a Buck's fizz, and is not too intoxicating.

EGGNOG

12 large eggs
1 lb castor sugar
½ pt bourbon

½ pt rum
¾ pt thick cream
grated nutmeg

Separate the eggs and beat the sugar into the yolks. When very smooth and creamy, beat in the bourbon and rum, little by little. Then beat in the cream gradually. Put in the refrigerator for 2–3 hours, then beat the egg whites until stiff, and fold into the mixture. Serve in glass bowls or short tumblers sprinkled with grated nutmeg. An extremely filling concoction, this drink really takes the place of a meal. Serves 10–12.

IRISH COFFEE

Have ready a jug of freshly-made strong black coffee, very hot; a bottle of Irish whiskey; $\frac{1}{2}$ pt thick cream straight from the refrigerator, and some castor sugar. The glasses should be warmed by filling with hot water and leaving to stand for 2–3 minutes. Into each one put:

I tsp sugar

a coffee cupful (4 fl oz) hot black
   coffee

a measure Irish whiskey

approx. I dessertspoon cream

Put the sugar in the warm glass and pour on the coffee. Stir until the sugar has melted, then add the whiskey and stir again. Hold a teaspoon upside down over the surface of the coffee and pour on the cream slowly, so that it floats on the top. Serve immediately.

A combination of dessert, coffee, and post-dinner drink, much loved by some, but a bit rich for my taste.